Discovering
the
True Love
Within

Christal M. N. Jenkins

Uncovering a Secret
Never Meant to be Kept Unknown

Xulon
PRESS

Cover by Michael Carson
Photography by Alisha Howard

Please visit my website at:
www.christaljenkins.com
Online ordering is available

Published by Christal M.N.Jenkins
Printed in the U.S.A

www.xulonpress.com

This book is dedicated to
Everyone who desires to discover MORE!

In loving memory of my grandmothers
Lillian Jenkins and Bette Jenkins

Special Thanks for your time and treasure in
support of this project:

Apostle Gary L. Wyatt Sr., Dr. Mark Strong,
Colleen Sterling-Williams, Pauline Hill, Moncella Young,
Erica Penton, Shawn Simmons
Brooke Brown, Dr. Katrina Hopkins (Tanner),
Stanley and Wanda Hopkins,
Jerry and Jolene Thomas, and Terri Dizard Cowley

Acknowledgements

There are so many people who have had a tremendous impact on my life. I could spend days trying to capture them all. So I would like to begin by saying "Thank You" to every person I've come across in my life. In some form or fashion, I celebrate you for being a part of my life and therefore this project.

To my parents—Christopher and Debra Jenkins: thank you for letting me "be me". For nurturing the gifts inside of me, and demonstrating your confidence in the principle, "Train up a child in the way they should go and when they get old they will not depart." I love you both!

To my siblings—Christopher II, Christian, and Christina Jenkins: I love you more than words can say. Each of you plays an intricate part in my life-past, present and future. I look forward to seeing us pursue the greatness for which God created us to be.

To the "First Family"—Alisha Howard and Jenelle Thomas: God only knew that as children, He was cultivating a sisterhood for a lifetime. The sisterhood we have has truly weathered every storm and I thank you for your encouragement, patience and most of all your love (Ecc. 4:12).

To my extended family—(grandmas, grandpas, aunties, uncles, cousins, nephews, nieces, etc.): Please know that you are truly loved. Thank you for being such a gift to my life. I pray daily that I represent you all well.

To all of my Godparents: Thank you for being my parents' extension of love, support and spiritual guidance. I truly thank God for each of you.

To my Devastating Sorors of Delta Sigma Theta Sorority Inc.: It is an honor to be a part of such a dynamic movement and legacy. Let us continue to go forth with the vision that was set before us. May God bless you all.

To all of "my Pastors": If I called you all out by name, it would be a long list. I am so thankful to God that each of you accepted the mantel that He placed on your life. Thank you for your Shepherd's heart, long-suffering and most of all being a vessel that He can use. I know that all of your best days are ahead of you!

To my extended church families: Thank you for your prayers, encouragement and support!

To Apostle and Mother Wyatt: Thank you so very much for allowing God to use you in the midst of your experiences. There is a river of life flowing out of me and I know I was called to be at a "Sure House" for such a time as this.

Last but not least, to my godchildren—Damien, Kaia, Mathias and Zora: Thank you for your unconditional love, and being the wonderful gifts that you are. Even as children you have truly demonstrated what it means to live a fruitful and abundant life. I know that God's purpose for you goes beyond your imagination! Each of you holds a special place in my heart.

Table of Contents

Preface

One Sunday I came home and felt led to write. I was not able to maintain a journal, so outside of writing small poems I had never written anything publish worthy. I sat on my bed with my laptop open. I told God "Lord here are my hands". As I began to type, the words flowed quickly from my head to my hands. I was overwhelmed by how God was using me. One week and five days later <u>Discovering the True Love Within</u> was written.

This book was written from the middle (part two), back to the beginning (part one), and then the end (part three). Part one is retrospective of my life up until the point I began my journey. Part two and three are more reflective and stylistically written differently in that they capture what God was revealing to me as I began to embark on my journey and walk into a new discovery of who He was.

I jokingly tell my family and friends that this book is Christal on paper. Some of my most vulnerable and intimate moments are unveiled in this book. I truly believe that by being transparent, this will allow others to see that they too can be whole and free. I have realized that the love of God has a way of destroying the masks and allowing me to experience the "fullness of joy and the pleasures forevermore"

So I invite you to join me as I take you through the genesis of my discovery of the TRUE LOVE within.

Christal M.N. Jenkins

Forward

In this rare extraordinary book for both women and men, Christal has done an outstanding job of sharing her own personal pain, process and discovery to reveal the true heart of God to us. Although she wrote this book in an 'unconventional' way, a way that most religious people will find difficult to read, it is the only way that this book could and should be written, since the God of love always does things in unorthodox ways, especially as it relates to revealing His love to us.

As I read the pages of her journey through pain and process it definitely shed a brighter light and built even more confidence in me that God indeed uses pain to mold and shape us into what He envisions and plans for us to be. The "Being Molded" chapter really enables one to understand that fire is absolutely necessary in becoming Gods new creation.

<u>Discovering the True Love Within</u> is high potency reading that will not only open your heart to the love process of God but it will also add fuel to the 'Grace Fire' that is needed to fully commit to the lifelong journey of discovering God's unfailing love.

I applaud, appreciate, and admire Christal for her boldness and candor in writing this book and her desire to see others discover God's true unconditional love. Without any reservations, I totally recommend Christal and this love provoking book to you and I hope and pray that as you read this book you, too, will let God's love for you reflect in your heart and your new love for God, reflect in His heart as well.

Apostle Gary L. Wyatt, Sr.

Introduction

Falling in love with Jesus is an experience like nothing I have ever encountered. His love is so pure, and accepting. Imagine, if you will, a love that doesn't hurt, reject or deny. Every insecurity, blemish, and imperfection is loved. I can be me, Christal, with all the issues and problems - the Christal no one really knows but the one God sees; the woman who felt so guarded and afraid of what it would be like to let go - to let go of the barriers and walls that had existed in my life for so long. It was a comfort to have these self-constructed mountains in my life. What do I mean by self- constructed?

Many of the mountains I experienced in my life were because of life. So many things I encountered both large and small had rooted into my heart creating small rocks. As life passed on, the small rocks were nurtured by other experiences that soon made them into mounds, and the mounds turned into hills and the hills then became mountains. I became so used to having them there that I didn't realize that they separated me from engaging in a true love relationship with God. I struggled with the concept of His love. Why does He love me so much? I know the biblical answers, but in my head I was trying to analytically comprehend the magnitude of a love that is not practical, but supernatural. I had experienced so much rejection in my life that True Love was a blur. I didn't believe I was a wounded soldier;

however, I thought that much of what I went through I had blown off and excused as not relevant or having any effect on who I was.

My perspective on life was molded and shaped by those very things I continued to overlook. Who I was becoming was carefully sculpted by family, friends, mentors and men. To my surprise, the strength I so exalted as a superior deity support in my life, was merely insecurity wrapped in fear. I guess you can say that I had a superficial understanding of God's love.

I had spent my entire life growing up in church. I had come to know who God was, and as a young girl I accepted Christ into my life. There was a power and a curiosity to come to know this man who had moved so many people. Why were Mommy and Daddy always crying and becoming so undignified over this man? They loved to talk about Him and my mother would get up in the wee hours of the morning just to pray to Him. I knew this was something great and I wanted to know Him also.

I remember the Sunday I stood in the aisle as everyone in the church was 'going crazy' in worship. In my heart I began to talk to God. I said, "If you can show me what you have shown them about who you are then I will serve you for the rest of my life."

You would think that a preschooler would not be able to articulate such a commitment. However, there was something unique about my request that day. Sure, I had learned about God's awesome power and His life in Sunday school; but the way Jesus was conveyed to me, I knew that there was something about "Jesus" that remained beyond my comprehension. So, as I stood in the aisle with a little tear coming down my face, I accepted Jesus into my heart, and to this day, I remember the joy I had after that encounter. I was so excited; I could hardly wait to tell everyone. I knew something great had taken place that day and I was ready to roll up my toddler sleeves and discover more about Jesus. My heart and mind was His and I had no problem with that.

Much of my life was spent dedicated to God. Why? Because I felt connected - I felt like I had purpose and my life made sense. I felt like I was accepted. Even still, God was only as big as I would let Him be. I spent time gaining knowledge of scripture and learning what it was that made God, God. By the time I was in grade school, many of my peers in church also had accepted Jesus and we were all very curious about our experiences. But in spite of their commitments, I always felt that mine was somehow different. I knew I was called to more.

j

Part One

Called to Be Great!

Purpose Unfolding

I was raised with a strong sense of self-pride. I learned to take pride in the family I came from, as well as the cultures and ethnic backgrounds of which I was a part. Through these lenses, I was able to see the world from various perspectives.

It was in discovering what the "more" was that made my pursuit of God personal. "Why me Lord?" I wanted to know why I was so special! You read in the Bible about David, Moses, Ruth, Hannah and others who were just ordinary people that were used in mighty ways; but what, besides the fact that God created me, made Christal Maria-Nicole Jenkins so great?

For many years as I was growing up, my mother home-schooled me and my two brothers. It was in these early years that I began to dream big dreams of what I could become. We had a huge play room with various stations for us to be creative and let our imaginations soar. As a young child I read the biographies of Thurgood Marshall and Barbara Jordan. I knew that I wanted to be a Supreme Court Justice just like him, or perhaps go into politics like Barbara Jordan, or maybe even have my own voice on TV like Oprah. I knew the world was mine, and all I had to do was decide what I wanted to do and go for it.

As a young girl I knew I was called to lead. I guess you could say I was the typical oldest child. Always in the front and always having something to say, I enjoyed taking charge and making things happen. I knew as a child, people could count on me. I always looked for ways to serve in any capacity. It was at a very young age that the gifts God had placed within me were being birthed and taking on life.

Having my gifts taken seriously at four years old was difficult at times. My mother had given birth to both of my brothers, and it was so important to me that my mom have a girl. After all, having a third boy would be detrimental to my livelihood! I wanted a little sister so badly! I remember being taught about the power of prayer and I was convinced that God would honor my request. He had to understand why my mother needed to have another child!

So every night I would go to bed praying for my baby sister, and every morning I would wake up and thank God for her. I did this for quite some time. I remember my mother saying she wasn't able to have anymore children, and even if it were possible, the doctor told her that her health and the baby's health would be in jeopardy. I didn't let that stop me! I was dedicated and motivated to see God answer my prayer.

In my family, I was used to watching God perform miracles so it had to be possible for God to give my mom another baby. He gave Mary, Jesus; He gave Hannah, Samuel, and He gave Sara, Isaac. So giving my mother another daughter and me a sister was a cinch.

One day we were all in the living room and my mother wasn't feeling well. I said, "Mommy, what's wrong?"

She said, "I think I have the flu."

I jumped up with joy and exclaimed, "I know what's wrong with you mom!"

She said, "What pumpkin?"

I said, "You are pregnant with my baby sister!"

She paused and looked at me like I was 'speaking in tongues.' Then she said in the most loving tone, "Mommy cannot have anymore babies." You won't get a baby sister but God has given you other sisters."

She began to list off my godsisters. I was not impressed. I said, "Yes you are, I know. I have been praying and God told me I was going to have a baby sister and she was going to be born in December."

Now this was around April of 1988. So my mom thought I was being 'so cute' and so did my dad. Even my family thought I was cute in my spiritual approach to requesting a baby sister. For me, this was more than a simple request. I knew what God had told me and what I had prayed for so diligently.

A week later my mother went to her doctor and, sure enough, the big news was that she was pregnant. My parents were dumbfounded! "Was this possible that our daughter had prayed another child into existence?"

I was overjoyed; I knew God and I had a special relationship and that He was going to move on my behalf. My sister, Christina, was born December 10th, 1988. That was my first encounter with hearing God's voice. Shortly thereafter, I was on the phone with my godmother and God told me to tell her that a blessing was on the way. She smiled and said, "Thank you baby." Sure enough, she got a new van that she needed that week. She called my parents in amazement!

People around my parents began to see the spiritual insight which was taking place in me. My mother, being the wise woman that she was, began to nurture the gifts in me. I didn't know that it was something supernaturally complex. I would hear it in my heart and believe what I heard. It was very simple to me. It was with that child-like faith I was able to grow closer to God in my youth. God was setting the stage for His purpose to be unfolded in my life; and these things provided a foreshadow of what my life was to become. My life was truly a gift and I looked onward with zeal and enthusiasm.

Closet Leper

Around the age of 14, I was diagnosed with a condition called "Alopecia Areata." It is a condition that tells your body that your hair follicles are harming the body. The immune system fights against the body's natural ability to grow hair by producing a swarm around the hair and killing it before it reaches the scalp.

It began as a small patch on the back of my scalp. I had so much hair when I was young that it was as if the patch were swallowed by the jet black glory I had been given. The condition came and then went. Then in middle school, the condition returned. I saw physician after physician and none of them could make a diagnosis. 'Maybe it was her thyroid,' one would say, or 'maybe it was a skin disorder.' The lack in diagnosis went on for some years, until finally it was discovered that I had Alopecia.

With that discovery, the doctors tried many medications to restore the hair loss. By this time the patches around my scalp had connected and were wrapping themselves around my head causing the lining of my hair to recede rapidly. Steroid crème was the first solution and it didn't work. Next, the doctor wanted to try steroid injections.

These injections inserted medication directly into my scalp to the affected areas and caused the swarm to disperse. We tried this solution and for a while, it worked. My hair began to come back—a patch at a time. I was overjoyed because being only 14 years old I could not imagine life without hair. I was just exploring my own identity and my hair provided me with the security I needed to continue to interact with my peers without being looked upon as sickly or different. I was afraid that I would not be liked or considered attractive without it.

Few people, if any, had heard of my condition and it was hard to tell people I didn't have leukemia or cancer. My condition is one reason that my heart goes out to people with those diseases. My illness was unique and less detrimental; yet, it still took an emotional toll on me. The days I would go in for treatment would be so taxing. I would have to wash my scalp and mentally prepare for what was ahead. As I sat in the examination room, the physician's assistant would be setting up the syringe and medication for the doctor. It seemed like everything was happening in slow motion. My heartbeat would beat louder and louder as I watched the preparation. The doctor would come into the room in his white jacket. He always had an 'awkward' smile on his face. I mean, who could come into a room with a huge smile knowing that you were about to puncture hundreds of tiny holes into someone's scalp?

His hands were always cold; even through the gloves I felt no warmth. He would look over my chart and ask me if I had seen any progress since the last visit. He would rub his hands gently over my scalp feeling the areas that had no hair to see if there were any changes. Once he had done his preliminary examination, he would walk over to the counter and begin preparing the medication. At times, watching the doctor fill the syringe made huge knots in my throat. After a while, I just got numb to the process because if I thought about everything that was going on I would have gone insane. I had to focus. I had scriptures I would ponder on as I sat in the room. Usually before the doctor would enter, my mother or father and I would pray together.

After the doctor or the assistant completed filling the syringes, he would roll the little tray near the bed. As I lay back on the bed, I remember thinking this procedure would make it all better. I only had to trust God that I would one day be healed. I lay my head back onto the thin paper covering the exam bed. The top of the bed was cool and I instantly felt it as my head touched.

I would look over to my mother and she would have this half smile on her face as she tried to hold back the tears. No mother wants to see her child in pain. She would always ask me if I needed her to hold my hand. Sometimes I would say yes, but after a while I was able to endure the pain alone. The doctor always used one hand to locate the spot with the gauze to prevent the seeping of blood, while the other hand held the syringe. I will spare you all the details of the insertion of the needle. I will say that afterwards, I had an alarming headache as well as gauze pads medically taped over my head to absorb the blood. There was a lot of head to cover since the disease had spread so quickly.

My head had gotten so bad that I looked like a sumo wrestler with a small patch on top. My aunt, being the fabulous hairstylist that she was, would put a weave ponytail on top of my head and gel down the hair around my afflicted areas to hide the hair loss. It worked very well! Even though I always felt like I was hiding something, I was able to go to school and no one would know what was happening underneath. It was much like my life; no one knew what I felt inside. It was a very lonely time for me.

It was hard to reach out to people because I had never felt this type of emotion before. I didn't even know how to articulate to others what I was truly feeling. On the one hand I was super strong because I believed that God would heal. On the other hand, I was insecure and very afraid of how people would respond if they really knew what was going on. I felt like a closet leper.

It was my freshman year at the school formerly known as Wy'east Jr. High. I was on the varsity basketball team. We had team photos on the 28th which I couldn't participate in because I had treatment that day. There would be no way I could go to the picture-taking session which was after school and have my hair taken down and head washed in time to be at my appointment on time. My appointments were booked months in advance because I had to see a specialist. I was crushed with missing the team photo and it saddened my teammates and me more than words can say. Fortunately, though, they understood.

On the morning of the photo shoot, I slept in because I didn't have to attend school. My parents had gone off to work, but my mother would be returning that afternoon to take me to the doctor's office. My siblings were all at school. I was home alone.

My bedroom was downstairs by the den. I had my own bathroom which was shared with our laundry room. I had to take my hair down and have it washed and be ready to go before my mother returned home. I avoided using my bathroom since I didn't have the things I needed there, so I quickly ran upstairs to my parents room to use their bathroom.

I gathered up the shampoo and conditioner from underneath the sink and sauntered to the hall closet to get a nice clean towel. I was ready to begin my regimen. I began by loosening up the hair on my head with a warm cloth, and then the gel. Once I had the gel loosened up, I was able to begin gently unwinding the ponytail on the top of my head.

As I unwrapped, loop after loop, I stared off into the mirror as if I did not recognize the person that it reflected. Could this be me? How could I be the one experiencing something like this. Each layer exposed more and more of my head. I was in awe at the state of my head. I could not believe it had gotten so bad. I was disheartened by the fact that I had to go through this and was frustrated that I saw little results. Why hadn't God just healed me? I continued to unwind slowly. Not wanting to jeopardize the small amount of hair left on my head, I was very careful in my approach.

As I got close to the end, I could see the ponytail now gracing the sink beneath me. I could feel the 'gooeyness' of the glue on my fingers. I had to concentrate even harder at this point. I knew that I had to be strategic about how I was to completely remove this last portion. As I gently began to tug on the last piece on the rubber band, I heard a small "creek" noise, almost like a snap.

Now I know what you are thinking...the rubber band broke. Well, yes it did, but it didn't break alone! I immediately looked down into the sink and I saw the rubber band *and* the ponytail, both lying inside the sink! What had just occurred didn't hit me right way; I hadn't quite realized what had happened! I looked up quickly and what I saw was so devastating, my emotions shut down—it was like I was truly looking at a foreign object in the mirror! Who was the bald woman I was staring at? The grimness of my question began to torment me as I played it *over* and *over* and *over* again in my head. Each time I could feel the rise of frustration stirring on the inside. I reached my hand up to touch the spot where hair once stood. The bare feeling sent chills down my spine!

NO! NO! NO! My heart screamed from the inside. As the reflection in the mirror became clearer, my eyes grew heavier and heavier. No! This is not happening! Why me! Here I am one week from my 15th birthday looking at myself in the mirror without any hair—just a matted patch on top from where the ponytail had been. How could I "face the music" now? There was no way I could be seen like this!

Feeling so alone, I had trouble processing what all of this meant in the moment. I stood in the silence of the bathroom with the light shining on my head like sunrays, and being too angry to even cry. I was faced with having to comprehend that I had experienced a loss so deep, that even my soul was screaming from within.

I felt like my life had ended in that one swift moment. What was I going to do? How was I supposed to live now? I had been born with gorgeous thick coal black hair. I had so much hair that my mother was constantly having to style it and take care of it.

My mind flashed back to my childhood and to all the times I hated getting my hair 'done' and not being able to play because I had to have my hair 'pressed' for church. What I wouldn't have given to have those moments back.

I was still numb and not fully accepting the reality that was in front of me. I had worked so hard to not allow my peers to be fully aware of what I was going through. I didn't want to be rejected. I didn't want to be seen by anyone; the humiliation was too much to bear. "What if my family was too embarrassed to be around me?" I thought. My poor brothers would get teased if people at school knew I had no hair. Then they would hate me for causing them so much grief. My cousin's big 15th birthday party was that weekend. All of her friends were going to be there. How embarrassing would I be to her if I showed up like this?

I just knew I was going to be alone forever! No guys would ever think I was beautiful ever again. I would be cast off and pushed to the side. I could not take the pain of having to live out this imaginative episode I was cultivating in my mind. I needed a way out, a way of escape. No one was home or around to help me. I was alone.

I began to shriek with anger! My eyes, no longer heavy, released the tears as they poured down my warm face. My hands began to swell from the impact of my locked grip on the sink counter. I was enraged!

All of these emotions were running rampant through my mind. I felt like I was dying a slow death and no one was there to witness it. I wanted to go away! I wanted my life to end! I could not take these feelings another second longer. I wanted out of my misery!

My eyes began roaming about the bathroom and I saw a knife on the far counter. I was sure my parents had a non-threatening reason for having the knife there, but for me, it was like I was staring my solution in the eyes. My mind immediately began to discover the possibilities. Death was like a sweet melodic tune in my ear for which I began to crave; I began to crave death; life no longer had meaning. For after all, I believed that God didn't care about me. If He did, why was I in this situation to begin with?

I grabbed the knife tightly. Overwhelmed with tears I could no longer see anything in front of me. I began to scream out loud to God. "Why, God why? I thought you loved me!"

As I continued to yell I could feel this demonic presence hovering over me. It was as if I were being taken over by something unfamiliar. My screams became more and more fierce and piercing! I could hear a voice in my ear urging me: "DO IT! DO IT!" The voice kept getting louder and louder! The pressure was simply too much to bear.

I pulled the knife to my chest and began to deeply push it into my skin. By now my clothes were drenched with sweat and tears. I was kneeling in a puddle of anguish. I yelled, "God if you are real, you better come save me because I am going to do it!" I repeated that statement as if the spirit that was trying to take over me was taunting God himself. I was becoming faint from the lack of oxygen that wasn't getting to my brain. I wanted to die, I wanted to die! I pressed in harder and harder. I yelled out again, "God..." but before I could finish, I felt this slight breeze move past my face. I noticed it immediately because I was so warm and overly exerted. I opened my mouth to yell once more. This time a still small sound was heard in the distance. Now I was already freaked out by the demonic presence that had taken over the room, but this small voice made me feel like I was in a twilight zone. Was this really happening? Was I going to wake up and find that all of this was a dream?

The demonic voice was trying to overshadow the interruptions: "DO IT NOW!" it yelled at me. "DO IT NOW!" The heaviness was beyond what I could control. I felt powerless and confused. Yet in the distance this voice was still there subtly coming closer and closer. I realized it was someone singing. In the midst of this chaos, my mind began to focus on this song. I heard the words, "You can make it; you can make it." Just as each breeze would go by I would hear the words to the song. The more I listened, the more I calmed down.

Tears began streaming uncontrollably; all I could do was cry! My vocal chords strained from the yelling; I couldn't even speak anymore. I cried silently alone. The song seemed familiar but it had been years since I had heard a song like that. "You can make it, you can make it, I don't care what you're going through, God's going to show you what to do; you can make it!"

My heart began to weep. I realized that I knew the song, but the voice I didn't recognize. It was almost angelic as it came and went with the breeze. Each time it came I felt a peace come over me. I felt the chills creeping up my back. The demonic voice that had yelled at me had ceased and it appeared as if the breeze were becoming stronger and stronger.

I realized that my hands were still clutching the knife. I was too afraid to let go. In that same terror, my mind was taken away from the room. I was in a large church sanctuary filled with people and all of my family was sitting in the front row. As I moved further back from row to row, the faces of the people were blurred. I couldn't see who they were. I was so frustrated by that. Where was I and why could I not see their faces?

As I surveyed the crowd once more, I noticed my family was weeping. I saw my nice, shiny oak casket with flowers on the top. I recognized that I had been taken to my funeral; but that still didn't explain the peoples' faces that I could not see! Then God said to me, "Those are the people your life has yet to reach; if you die now they will never be reached!" I wept even harder. I saw the brokenness on the faces of my family and I realized that my life had meaning, that there was more than what I was making it out to be. I had to live!

I suddenly realized what a scene it would have been for my mother to return home to take me to my appointment, only to find me lying in a pool of blood, sink full of hair, and no one to explain how this all came to be. The devastation she would have felt! She would question if she had come home a moment sooner, perhaps her baby girl would have been saved! Wondering whether she could have done something to prevent what happened?

My siblings would have been rushed home from school only to find their big sister was dead! No explanation, no letter—nothing but a dead body! The conclusion would have been more piercing than the knife that killed me if they'd discovered that I had died from a broken heart.

Eyes of the Beholder

Insight

It was difficult for me to comprehend everything that just happened upstairs in my parent's bathroom. One thing was clear—I was still alive! But what did that all mean? What was I suppose to do now? I slowly got up off the floor and threw the knife off to the side. I looked at myself in the mirror, still mourning the loss I had just suffered. I slowly gathered up the hair from the sink. I would normally wash out the hair and let it dry so that I could reuse it, but this time I leaned over reaching for the cabinet beneath. I pulled out the garbage bin and placed the contents of my hands inside. I didn't want to let go but I knew I had to loosen my grip.

My heart ached with a pain I had never felt before. Even knowing that my life had meaning didn't change how I felt. Remaining in my head was the thought of how was I going to "face the music"? I finished straightening up the bathroom and then grabbed the shampoo. It was as if I were a robot as I began to wash and condition my head. Tears were flowing subtly and slowly down my face.

I spoke no words, I just stared. I thought to myself, "Christal, this is you now. This is you." As I dried my head, I wondered what my doctor and my aunt would think now. We all had high hopes that this day would never come.

Would they feel defeated? I didn't want to see the remorse on people's faces as if I had some shameful disorder. I didn't want people feeling bad or sorry for me.

Walking back down the stairs, I knew I had to do something fast to renew my mind. I ran down to my room and grabbed my Bible, but I couldn't even think of a scripture to read so I ran back up to the living room and turned on the TV. I flipped quickly to TBN and sat still. "This is Your Day" with Benny Hinn had just come on the air. I softly chuckled to myself at the irony of the program. I looked on attentively hoping that Benny would point out my direction and prophesy of my healing. That never happened. Sarcastically, I wasn't disappointed at all. I mean, why would I expect that to happen to me? Nonetheless, I was encouraged by the testimonies of others. As he read letters from people who sent in their testimonies, I drifted off into my Bible.

I quietly asked the Lord to show me something, to give me some hope, and He led me to James 1:2 *"Consider it pure joy, my brothers, when you face trials of many kinds for the testing of your faith develops perseverance and perseverance must complete its work. That way you may be perfect and complete not lacking anything".*

It was in those words that I gained insight. I wondered what had occurred in James' life for him to write those words in the beginning of his book. That was his opening mantra. I felt inspired by his words; it had a way of bringing consolation to me in the midst of the storm in which I found myself.

I figured God must have really liked me enough to allow this to happen to me. I recognized that I was going through a process. I didn't understand at the time the real meaning of perseverance, but I just knew I had to have *Joy*. I knew Joy was deeper than happiness; Joy had to come from within. Where was I going to conjure up this joy? I knew it was something God was going to have to give me. I needed His strength now more than ever.

Glimpse of Hope

I continued with my treatments. As painful as they were, I felt they were the only way I could have my hair comeback. I went on to high school the next year, and by this time I had found security in wearing hats. My father spared no expense in making sure I had the proper coverings for my head. I had bandannas in every color you can imagine, and I had hats of all kinds. My dad even shaved his head, so I would not be the only one in the house without hair. Let me be clear though, he did have a bald spot forming on the top, so he may have had a little extra motivation to follow through with his new hair style.

In the winter quarter of my sophomore year, I finally saw a glimpse of hope! The treatments had taken full form and my hair was making a comeback. My hair returned just in time for the winter dance. I was so excited! I had the Jada 'slick back' hair style. It was cute and people really received the hair style change. Soon thereafter, I felt the need to relieve myself from the burden of going every month to the doctor for the injections. With the emotional duress I constantly endured from going to my treatments, you must understand why, after my hair had grown back, I rushed to stop the treatments.

It was wonderful to wake up and put moisturizer in my hair, brush it down, and run out to my bus. My hair was fine like the hair of a baby; I loved its softness as I gently rubbed my fingers through it. I would always look into the mirror and smile. I knew my hair was my glory and it was so awesome to see God restore what was once completely gone. I didn't take it for granted because my experience was so fresh in my mind.

It was so exciting to tell people how God had used modern medicine to cure my disease. Rarely do people who have the condition for as long as I did, get their hair back. Many people who suffer from Alopecia lose not only the hair on their head, but also their facial hair and some have complete body hair loss. I felt extremely blessed.

The excitement was short-lived and over time the spots started to re-appear. They began as tiny spots, so I would just apply crème to them to medicate the small patches; but soon the patches began to grow again.

My parents didn't want me to feel as though I had to go back to treatments. They wanted it to be my decision. Since it had proven to work before, I was willing to endure the pain to obtain the same results. I continued the treatments for a while, and then just called it quits. I realized that God was a healer, I wanted to rely on Him, and I wanted to take a break for a while. My peers had accepted the state I was in, so I felt comfortable enough not to continue. I knew I was running the risk of letting my condition becoming untreatable but I had made up my mind.

Seeing Myself

Thus began my first discovery of seeing me in a new way. I was forced to deal with these new changes and I adjusted to my new lifestyle. It was during this transition that God began to show me how *He* saw me. This was new to me because I always believed that I saw myself in my own way. I thought that I never really cared that much about the opinions of others, other than my family's and closest friends.

Now, understand that I didn't see a great deal when I saw myself. I realized I had never really known who I was before the hair incident. I was challenged with the fact that I now had to see me. What does it mean to see me? I thought of my past and tried to piece together some things, only to discover that there were a number of pieces missing. My life was like a puzzle and with each experience I encountered a new piece. God was connecting each piece together as time moved forward.

I knew that I had to reach out to find what I was missing. I needed to figure out who I was now, as no person wants to walk around aimlessly without any direction. Uncovering who I was allowed me to find peace in what was now my life.

Even though I had a smile on my face, I felt alone on the inside. In trying to contemplate who I was, and looking at myself in the mirror, it showed only a little pinch of the immense pain. I had accepted that the reflection staring back at me from the mirror was indeed me, but I wondered how I would gather the pieces of the puzzle that made me.

I held fast to James 1:2 like a dog gnawing on a bone. I had to constantly remind myself I was being perfected. It had a melodious ring to it that I liked hearing. I was encouraged to continue on.

It was during one of my emotional 'fits' with God that I realized that the person I saw was not the same person God saw. "Why did He see differently than me?" I thought.

I was mesmerized by the fact that God had different lenses and how, on the one hand, despite my outward appearance, he really saw the woman that he had made. He was not taken back by my lack of hair; He was hurt by my lack of self-worth.

How could something God made so beautifully, be something I could have thought was so ugly? I hated, at times, how I looked because it was hard for me to see beauty among what I thought was ashes.

It was hard for me to change my perspective because I had to first acknowledge that during the course of my life what I valued for myself was very shallow and superficial. No one wants to admit that their self-perception is in some ways superficial, but it was the only conclusion that I could have drawn at the time.

Changing lenses

I had no choice but to reconstruct my self image. That wasn't an easy task and I really wasn't as motivated as I should have been. I knew that I had to do it regardless of my feelings. I could not continue to have these random 'fits' and 'pity parties'; my life had to go on.

I began to read Psalms 139 where David described in poetic detail the wonder of God's creation. David spoke to his existence, and concluded that he was fearfully and wonderfully made. I wondered whether David was questioning his own self worth when he wrote that Psalm. I wondered if he were speaking to himself, about himself, to encourage himself.

I decided that I was going to establish myself on the foundation of how God viewed me. I was no longer going to wallow in shame, at least not any time soon! I was going to move on with my life. After all, it was just HAIR!!! So much worse had happened to people—I needed to get a grip. So, I did!

Yes, I know you may be thinking: "Oh it was very easy for you to move on." Actually, it was not as simple as it was put. Just because I was able to get a grip did not mean that I dealt with all the issues behind my insecurities. They did not come from only losing my hair. My insecurities were there all along; they surfaced because of my hair loss.

There were so many other things I had to consider in my life; I knew focusing and worrying about my hair was getting me no where. I was never one to throw my own pity party and invite guests; I never showed up when my friends invited me to theirs and I was determined not to begin at this time!

A New Day

The sun will come out tomorrow

Growing up, one of my favorite movies aside from 'Lady and the Tramp' was 'Annie'. I loved her story. I could watch that movie over and over and still be moved by the ending. I even had the Annie doll. It was something about Annie's life that spoke to me. Here was this young girl in search of her parents. All she wanted was to belong and to have a place to call home. The interesting part to this story was that while Annie was searching for her real parents, she found herself on a journey to find out who she was as well.

Her determination to find out where she came from would allow her to know more about herself. She was not giving up and it was in that moment when it seemed dark and grim that she sang, "The sun will come out tomorrow!" My favorite part of the song was

"When I'm stuck in a day
That's gray,
And lonely,
I just stick out my chin
And grin,
And say,
Oh

39

The sun'll come out
Tomorrow
So ya gotta hang on
'Til tomorrow
Come what may
Tomorrow!
Tomorrow!
I love ya
Tomorrow!
You're always
A day
A way!"

Annie reminded herself that no matter what she was experiencing that day, she was always looking ahead knowing that tomorrow would bring new hope, and opportunities. Tomorrow was only a day away. It was the hope of the new day that kept her sane in her 'today.'

Much like Annie, I too, had to persevere to the new day with hope that in each new day, I would uncover more and more that would lead me to discover who I was.

Kick Back

My discovery continued to unfold as I went on throughout my high school years. Much of my "deliverance" was masked in my peers and church. I'd reached a point where I felt like I needed to reach out beyond the church I was attending. Much of my life had been spent there, and I was ready for a transition. A friend of mine from school invited me to her church. I was excited to go; I mean, I was always 'down' to go to church, so I went with her.

I was in awe by the intensity of the worship and the 'Word.' I felt like this was a place I wanted to be. I was so free to worship God in a new way and the services were led by young people. It was great to see another church where gifted young people were put in positions of leadership and encouraged to 'stir up' the gifts inside of them. At my church my youth pastors were transitioning to other roles within the church. I felt as if this were my time to branch out, see what else was out there, and to see what other churches had to offer. I wasn't much of a 'church hopper.' I was the type to stay in a church until I felt God was moving me elsewhere.

I went to the new church only for youth group. I still enjoyed the Sunday services at my current church and wasn't ready to trade in the entire experience. I had the blessing of my pastor to be a part of this other ministry, so I went.

The atmosphere was fun; they had a much larger youth group than what I had experienced in the past. The church was rather large so the youth ministry truly reflected that expanse as well. Some of the youth came only to youth church. They were young people from the area and they were just gaining an understanding of who God was. To them, youth church provided a safe haven to meet up with friends and 'hang out.' What parent could argue with their child about going to church?

All in all, youth church on Wednesday nights was the place to be when we were in high school. No one wanted to 'miss out!' I made a lot of new friends and enjoyed building new relationships. I even reconnected with my childhood best friend. We picked up right where we had left off. The experience paid for itself!

Every summer there was a youth camp called "Kick Back"; it was out at this nice 'campsite' that had cabins and dormitories. It came with a large chapel that had a full sound system and musical instruments, as well as a full service kitchen and staff. Also, the wave runners for our days at the water made this the place to be in the summer time. Kick Back was our place to escape life as we knew it and to spend a week with God and our friends. Who could have asked for a better vacation?

It was at this camp that I experienced a transformation. Each night changed my life more and more. Could this be possible? Experiencing so much growth in such a short time seemed unreal! Most of the young people were so absorbed in the experience; they recommitted their lives to God every summer. Not to make light of anyone's commitment, it was just understood that you would not leave camp the same way you came!

Each night, I became more and more comfortable. In worship, I used to get so hot until my bandanna would stick to my scalp from the sweat. I would occasionally take it off during worship since everyone was focused on God and few people were in position to stare at me. I would ring out my bandanna and put it back on in time for the Word. I found myself still not sure about completely letting go. After all I did have a nice shaped head and my close peers didn't seem to be taken aback by my appearance.

It was the night at the bonfire that changed things forever. People were coming down to the front sharing all that God had done in them during the week. I sat there feeling the inner urge to talk about how I was going to allow God to free me from the shame I carried with my disease. I wanted to make a statement and burn up my bandannas as a sign that I no longer had to hide behind them. When I finally got the courage to walk down, I could hear people cheering as I walked closer to the front. I was encouraged by everyone's anticipation of what I was going to say.

I began to share my story with them about my condition. I shared my personal struggle and how being at camp made me feel that God was setting me free from things I had been dealing with since my condition took over. I felt so empowered by the attentive looks on everyone's face and by the tears, for many people even cried. I was like, "Yes! This is what I was supposed to do." So for my closing, I ripped off my bandanna as a sign that I would no longer wear them because I did not have to use them as a comforting blanket anymore.

Everyone cheered, people began standing up and the applause grew stronger. I felt such a sense of accomplishment. I was so thankful to God for the courage to say what I said.

For the rest of the week, I did not wear my bandannas. It felt great! I wasn't even concerned over the huge sunburn on my head from doing camp activities in the field. I guess that was life without covering on my head! Therefore, I rejoiced and exuded extreme joy when I returned home from camp.

My parents were very pleased with the testimony I shared with them about my experience. Even people at church received it well, on the Sunday after camp, when I wore nothing at all to shield my head.

It was amazing the freedom I felt. I no longer had to be held captive by the lies that I was told by the enemy. The humiliation was gone and I was now finally able to cope with who I was physically. I was able to look in the mirror with a smile, and not be afraid of what people were thinking.

I was grateful to God for what he had done in me during that week. I knew I still had a long road ahead of me, but at least I had reached a landmark. I had left some things behind never to look back.

Taking a Break

My senior year of high school was a very interesting one. I had spent the last six years of my life dedicated to ministry: learning, teaching, preaching and serving. I reached a point where I wanted to take a back seat for a while. Now, I just wanted to receive! I spent much of my youth pouring and pouring and pouring, and using my personal devotion as a means to get full again. I wanted something deeper; I was tired of the mundane that had resulted from my continual service.

I knew I wasn't going to get off the hook that easily but I was determined to try. I knew that people had high expectations as to what I could do beyond my secondary years. After all, on my high school campus, I started a Bible study that grew to be the largest Bible study that campus had ever seen. Classrooms were packed during both lunches. I set up a leadership team that could minister during lunch hours and I brought in guest youth pastors to speak once a month. It was great to see people who wouldn't normally go to church come spend their lunch experiencing what God had in store for them.

Aside from that, I remained in leadership roles at my own church and occasionally spoke at small youth events. Also, I was a member of the Senior Class Council at my school; at the same time, I tried to be a "normal" teenager.

Sure, I did normal teens things such as work for McDonalds, go to the movies, go to all the high school games and hang out on weekends with my friends. Balancing all of this seemed normal to me, since I had never taken time to think about it all.

Doing all of these things kept me out of trouble. I wasn't running behind boys like my peers or getting caught up in 'drama'. I was just 'doing me'. I knew people counted on me to be an example, so I felt I had to surrender to the pressure and conform to the image they desired. It was difficult for me to watch people not uphold standards and principles. Being double- minded was not an option for me. I had to walk 'straight'.

I was very social so I had a lot of associates, but very few friends; my circle was small. Many people around me thought they were my friends but I could count on one hand how many friends I really had. Because of the various roles

I had, I didn't need people all in my business. Sadly to say, though, there were always 'haters' trying to find some reason to destroy my character. Obviously, the haters had nothing better to do!

As I approached graduation on my way to the University of Washington (UW), I was excited by the idea of becoming invisible again. Being someone that hid in the crowd and not having to carry such a heavy mantel around, I could explore some unknown territory and create a new lifestyle for myself. It was my time to take a break from the life I had once been a part of, and reconstruct a new blueprint that I could then build and live by. It was mine to own; no one could make me do otherwise!

I remember having lunch with my pastor at the time and one of my "big sisters". I proudly talked about my new plans and he quickly shot them down. He told me that I was not destined to fit in with the crowd. Since my name meant 'the light,' no matter what I did, I would always shine above the rest. I hated the very notion he was suggesting. I felt he had underestimated my abilities to be whom and what I wanted.

I laughed off his comments and continued to eat my lunch. Could what he was saying be true? I hope not, I thought. I was absolutely drained by the leeches I had inherited while being in ministry, especially the people who selfishly sucked you dry only to wind up co-dependent and never taking heed to the support you provided. I was tired of always having to be on my 'A' game everywhere I went, always under the microscope of the world! I wanted to be like "Waldo" so hidden that unless I wore my red and white striped shirt no one could find me. I didn't want to have this subterfuge forever - just for a while, until I could get my bearings - just long enough for me to adjust to being a normal student in a new city.

I was the type of person who wanted to skip high school for college. I felt that high school was more social than academic and it was always filled with 'drama' and immaturity. Girls thinking that *Prom* was the defining moment to sell themselves short only to wind up unloved and rejected, and glorifying an experience that only caused mutual desolation and resentment. Or, people assuming that they were their parents' future financial investment.

In other words, I believed that they were all going to graduate into a world that could care less, and instead of pursing their dreams, they would run away to their safe haven and accept mediocrity as a way of life.

So, all in all, I couldn't wait to graduate. I was ready for what the world had to offer. I had made up in my mind as to what I was going to do. I knew I would eventually be like so many others and change the world. I thought I could do it one law at a time. I loved to debate and discuss, so being in Law was my life-long dream. In elementary school, as I mentioned studying the life of judges, I would also job-shadow judges and anticipate walking in their shoes. Even my soccer coach was a district court judge. I was ready to put years and years of dreams into action. In order to do so I felt I needed to readjust my priorities. So I went off to college in hopes of leaving everything behind, and moving forward to what lay ahead.

An Awakening

Tough Questions

College provided me with an opportunity to self assess on another level. It was a new environment with unfamiliar people and the comfort I had known growing up back at home was now gone. I had to start fresh, become open to new relationships and experiences.

My freshman year, I had a relationship that seemed to always run up against the same walls. He was frustrated with the way I communicated. He was so 'intense' and always very open and he desired to show his affection toward me. After awhile he would come around I would try to avoid him. I couldn't understand why he wanted to engage in such a serious relationship with me. I never took relationships seriously. I was under the mantra that I never wanted to be hurt. So I lived my life closed and unattached from people, mainly men. He would always say, "Let's talk." The strange thing was we were always in a discussion when he would say this. I didn't understand what he was saying to me, so my instant response was always anger and frustration. I would lash out and say, "What are you talking about; we have been talking for the past hour!" I began to get annoyed with this constant interruption in our conversations. "What in the world was his problem?" I thought. "What else does he want?"

Of course he could not explain what he meant without going into another hour-long discussion. So it was safe to say that I, who talked all the time, spent the majority of my time not trying to talk. I was at the point where I felt I could no longer provide him with what he needed. So I let the relationship die. To most people, this guy was someone any girl would love to be with. However, the more he continued to press me emotionally, the more I ran away. What was it that bothered me? Why was I so afraid of what he was asking? At the time I was in no place to try to understand; I was a college freshman with the world to discover. I could not be tied down by some guy who wanted all of my attention and interest. I just assumed his issues were beyond my support, or so I thought. I convinced myself that he was the problem, and that I would end up in a horrible relationship if I pursued this.

His questions haunted me even after he moved away. What was it about this relationship that struck such a chord in me? I spent the remaining year in other relationships that never were as in-depth as the first. I was dumbfounded by the concept of communication or the lack there of. I was the queen of gab and never had a problem with any other guy making such 'illogical' requests.

It wasn't until my sophomore year of college that I really came face to face with what I had been avoiding my entire life. I was in my neighbor's room in the dorm. She and I were having a conversation and I was venting about my current relationship woes. During our discussion I made a statement with all confidence: "I will never ever be hurt in a relationship; I will leave before I let that happen."

At the time, my friend had just returned from the washroom and was putting her clothes away in her closet. She paused and laid her shirt down on her pillow. I wasn't sure what she was doing. She looked at me in the eyes and said nothing. Then a short moment later she said, "How would you know what you are protecting yourself from, if you have never been hurt?"

At first without truly listening to what she was saying I said, "What are you talking about?"

She replied, "You said you had never been hurt, so how can you know how to avoid being hurt unless you have been hurt before?"

That question was like a bullet through my heart. I wasn't sure how to answer the question. What was I protecting myself from all of these years? I had never been violated or abused by anyone; my life experiences were full of love and life. So what was I so afraid of? What was I working so hard to protect? I know the scripture said, "Guard your heart" but I was barricading my heart, and why?

I left the room feeling worse than when I went in. I couldn't wrap my head around what it was that made me so cold and distant. Sure, I had friends reject me or backstab me in times past, but I was always leery of men and pain. I went back to my room and sat on my bed.

I spent weeks rewinding my life, going through those memories that never possessed the answers to my questions.

It was not until I began to reflect deeper on my past, looking beyond the surface that my childhood began to unlock a key that provided much needed answers to my tough questions.

Daddy's Girl

Bishop T.D. Jakes is a television evangelist. I remember watching one of his sermons one day and he said that a woman's first encounter with a man is with her father. That statement held both weight and truth. After all, in the many discussions I have had with women, I found that most of their issues traced back to their fathers or the lack there of. I never related this precept to my personal life because I grew up in a 'Cosby like' household. Both my mother and father were well educated, spiritually 'saved' (not just in church but in the home), and exhibited a loving marital relationship. I had what most of my peers never had.

As a child I was the 'apple' of my daddy's eyes. I was a very proud daddy's girl. I can remember after my mom put us to bed, I stayed awake until I heard daddy's footsteps coming through the door after work. I would sneak out of bed and run to greet him at the door. He always had a special treat for us. I always got first pick!

I looked up to my father. He was very well known in the community; aside from his education he was also a preacher. I loved being around my dad! He was always quoting scriptures, singing "songs of Zion" and engaging in deep analytical discussions. People would say that I was just like my dad. We do have very similar personalities - after all, my dad did go into an 'all night shut-in' (prayer meeting) praying that my mother would have a girl first and that she would be just like him. When I tell you God answers prayer, you have no idea! It's safe to say I should have been the "junior" in the family.

Church was the common denominator between my father and me. We both had a strong devotion and love for God, so we always connected when it came to the things of God. My parents always taught me to think things through thoroughly and ask questions much, like in 'all your getting, get an understanding.' My father and I would engage in intense biblical and analytical conversations. These discussions were always challenging and forced me to have substance to back up any response I had.

Some times when I would get disciplined, he wanted to have a five-hour discussion on the biblical relevance to my situation and why my actions had both practical and spiritual consequences. It was during those times I would have rather been grounded or even spanked to be put out of my misery! He always had this way of getting his point across without having to yell; his voice was stern! Yet even in the meek tone of his voice you would know this was a very serious matter.

I adored my father; he could do no wrong. No matter what; it didn't matter; my daddy was my hero! I knew I felt secure and comfort being around him and knowing that he would always be there. There is something in every woman that yearns to be a daddy's girl. Even as an adult, I find myself enjoying the security of my father's love. No matter what I did - whether, I wrecked his car, didn't do my chores, or got in trouble at school, my father always showed his unconditional love even through his disappointment.

My daddy's love made me feel like a princess in the castle of life. I felt like I could accomplish anything! The world was mine to own and I was going to pursue it with all diligence.

Breaking Through

It wasn't until my junior year of college that I truly realized the answer to my heart's secret delusion. The mystery of what made me so complex, and why I was so afraid to discover those hidden truths. Psychologically, I had forced out any memory that appeared to be unpleasant and or painful as a mean to self- soothe and process life. I had developed a sense of pride for the strength I could assert in any situation, and I convinced myself that showing any emotion was a sign of weakness which would pierce through my hard shell and allow vulnerability to seep out like a toxic gas.

I avoided any situation that could jeopardize my delusional reality, potentially putting me at ease as I went through life knowing that my false sense of security would never be tainted. It was under these pretenses that it took me a great deal of time to realize I was in essence emotionally on the defense in life, not on the offense. What was it that had triggered this defense? Unlocking this mystery was so traumatic that I had many sleepless nights, allowing my mind to be taken on a journey of pain that I never anticipated.

What could be so painful you might ask? The Truth!

Now, I am not saying that my entire life was a lie, but my personal assessment of my life was merely skewed with what I wanted, and didn't want to be real. So, to ensure that I never had to face the facts, I hid them away so deeply inside that no one, not even me, could go back and reclaim them.

I am sure by now you are anticipating this really horrible truth to unfold, but in actuality the revelation was simple. I had experienced a lot of hurt and rejection early in life that forced me to tuck myself into a fetal position of fear, and build a barricade around myself. As I began to process my life, I reflected on my childhood, and realized that I had suppressed a lot of things to save face.

It was simple. I felt as though my feelings weren't justified because I had not experienced situations that most of the women I encountered in life had faced. However, the common thread among some of these women and me was that I had the same feelings they had: the rejection, the lost sense of self, indescribable pain, and a loss of security. The only problem was that because my situation was not as clearcut, I saw myself as being ungrateful and overly emotional about what I was feeling and experiencing.

Being such a die-hard daddy's girl had its perks, and its detriments. As I grew older my relationship with my father began to change dramatically. In my mind, he was preoccupied with so many things in life—career, providing for his family, church leadership responsibilities and learning how to be a father, that our connection got lost among the' crowdedness' in life.

Much of my dad's life was spent in the social work arena where he worked with many children who didn't have the family I had. He dedicated his life and time to mentoring, counseling, supporting, and praying for them, which meant that as life went on, it appeared that when he returned home, he didn't have much of anything left to give to us.

Nothing, absolutely nothing was harder than watching my father being a father to everyone else and feeling as if my birthright was rejected. To me, it felt as though it happened overnight. Broken promises, lack of quality time and lack of visibility took precedence. My mom being the woman that she was always tried to step in and make up for the lack, but it wasn't enough for me. I wanted my daddy back! I could see him, but couldn't touch him, and the realities of seeing people have a closer relationship with my father than I had, were really painful. What about me? What did I do wrong?

I knew I couldn't speak up much about it because it would appear that I was complaining. I thought, well at least I *have* a dad. I felt guilty and selfish for even petitioning such a thought. I thought about all the people that needed him outside of me and so I just kept everything inside. I was broken by the fact that he always seemed to have time for other people but never for me.

I tried to include my dad in my life on many occasions but no occasion seemed to fit into his schedule. Being a young woman trying to discover my own identity, I found myself looking elsewhere for attention. Yes, my mother raised me to be a woman, but my needing my father's influence to provide me with a sense of identity and belonging that only a man could provide seemed absent. I had this sense of wanting to be noticed. I had a loss of security and acceptance. I was rejected by the one man who was supposed to make me feel the most important thing in life outside of God.

As I began to relive moments of my childhood I was overwhelmed by the amount of experiences my mind could conjure up, and it broke my heart all over again. I recalled that at one point I stopped caring about even wanting a relationship with my dad and just grew cold. I numbed myself with lies to make me feel better. I had pretended not to care for so long, that I actually believed it never bothered me.

I wanted to reach out to other "dads" in my life but they seemed to reject me for many of the same reasons as well. I felt like I just got lost or overlooked most times. There was one place where I never felt overlooked, that was in church. Since the age of 12, I served in leadership at my church. Serving God through ministry was my only outlet. I enjoyed working with youth and supporting ministries was so natural for me. Through ministry, I was provided with a feeling of security and being needed.

I was faithful and served with all due diligence. I felt a sense of accomplishment in being able to see peoples' lives changed; I knew God was pleased, and I didn't want Him to ever reject me.

As I continued on in ministry, people would say, "She is just like her dad." I would love hearing those words because that was the only time I felt most connected to him. I vicariously had a relationship with my earthly father through doing work in the church for my Heavenly Father.

Some would say this might seem to be an extreme depiction for something so common, but the truth has that affect at times. I managed to fully indulge myself until it became the premise for my mere existence. Sure, destiny had its place, and I was well aware of my call to ministry and evangelism' but much of my experience was convoluted by my desire to feel loved.

The reality was that I had become so numb that the only time I was vulnerable was in God's presence. I had locked myself away so that I could not make connections deep enough to hurt me. I had been so focused on never being hurt that I forgot the reason I was protecting myself to begin with — until that night in the dormitory.

I am sure you may be thinking, "Isn't that a lonely existence?" Honestly, it can be, but for me having only God to truly depend on was the melodic chorus of my life. Again, I lived under a second mantra of "as long as I got Jesus, I don't need nobody else".

Yes I know that people and relationships are important, and that is not to say that the ones I had built, I didn't have a vested interest. It was that the love and energy I gave to them was on a long, tight-rope, meaning just enough so that they feel close, but not enough so that I could get hurt. This way of thinking became so ingrained and systematic, I never thought about it until college. I never questioned why I did much of anything that involved my emotions. The true understanding of the answer to this question I tried to subconsciously avoid.

So what was it that I was trying to break through? Much of what I realized would take years of therapy to undo, and being a child of a psychotherapist just seemed like a journey I didn't want to embark on. I knew that I had to get past this experience if I ever was to be able to one day know what true love was about. How could I say I loved my children or my husband, if I never experienced love without restrictions?

Matters of the Heart

It was in the moments of the past year that I was able to process the matters of my heart for the first time since I was a child. It was bittersweet in the sense that I was becoming free, but yet in order to do so, I had to come face to face with the pain.

As I sat in my room in my apartment, I was reminded of a missionary trip when my father took me and my siblings to Baja, Mexico. Our church was headed down to partner with other churches on a three-day pastoral retreat for the pastors and their families from Mexico.

I reflected on one of the nights my father was sharing his testimony with the Mexican youth. He was talking about his relationship with my grandfather. He told of how he felt rejected and had a lost sense of security growing up feeling like he was never wanted. He had to watch my grandfather raise someone else's children while he and his sisters struggled living alone with their mother.

My father told the group of the times he would walk down the street to 'this' house and look up at the bedroom window feeling so hurt and frustrated about the situation, he just wanted to go inside and pull his daddy out and take him home.

As my father told the story, he had tears coming down his eyes. We could 'hear a pin drop' as the young people were listening attentively to my father's story being retold by the translator. It was so powerful! My daddy has always had that affect on people when he spoke.

My dad continued with how he was able to be free from his pain by finally speaking to his father after my grandmother had passed away. He said he knew he had to release it so that he could move on. He acknowledged that the bottled up emotions had a direct reflection on how he interacted with his wife and children. He spoke of the barriers in love that he had because of his pain.

That night after my father spoke, the altar was full of young men and women who had felt led to release to God what they were feeling on the inside. These were pastors' children who could relate to my father's story.

As I watched from a distance, I was unable to make a connection with the experience. I saw it as an awesome 'ministry time' and was amazed at my father's boldness and vulnerability. I did not appropriately connect my pain to that of my father's directly. I realized that we had similar feelings but mine were so repressed that I soon forgot about them after that moment and wiped them clear from my mind.

That night in my apartment, I made the connection for the first time. I cried like I had never cried before. It felt strange, but yet a sense of comfort to cry. It had been forever since I allowed myself to cry more than a few brief tears. I recognized that I, too, had to get free or my children would have to experience the devastating results of a generational curse that had not been broken. I didn't want another generation to have to experience what I and past generations had experienced.

The matters of the heart can be so delicate, and once tapped into, they can have an overwhelming reaction. I found myself, a young adult, finally untangling the chains that had me in bondage most of my life. I now had to decide what I should do with what I had uncovered. Could I allow my time of grief and relief to be my reality end-all, and allow myself to move on past it?

Many years had passed. Bringing up such issues at this point in my life seemed unnecessary, especially since my father and I had found a way to maintain a relationship in spite of my detachment. He had grown to be a wonderful father; my younger sister was able to have the daddy I always wanted my entire life. It was a blessing to watch him grow. So why would I selfishly throw my issues in his face years later. How unfair could that be to him? I thought. What if he really rejects me even more for accusing him of not being there and having the relationship I needed to ensure that I grew up emotionally attached?

I contemplated these things for days. I would daydream in class wondering what I should do. I couldn't tell my friends out of embarrassment that it would bring shame to my family since I thought I was being 'over the top.' I was retreating back to what had me bound in the first place—suppressing my feelings and emotions, and denying their validity and importance. The back peddling was sending me into a place of torment that I didn't need nor want to experience.

The Letter

After a few sleepless nights, I had to pour out everything that was on my mind. My brain was going a mile a millisecond, and I had to stop the relay before it killed me. I awoke out of my sleep one night, jumped out of bed, and quickly sat down to my desk. I grabbed a pen from my drawer, and opened up to the middle of one of my subject notebooks. I began to write "Dear Daddy..." As I wrote, tears flooded my eyes. In the immediate, I had no intention of sending the letter. I just wanted to write as if I were talking to him. It was very late by the time I completed the letter. Most of the words looked like 'chicken scratch' and some of the ink was blurred by teardrops. I had finally gotten out of my head what I had been carrying in my heart for years. It was so freeing! I lay down in my bed and slept like a baby that night.

The remaining resolution was what I should do with the letter. So as not to lose any of the substance that I had captured the night before, I carefully rewrote the letter so that it was clear. That next weekend I went home to visit my parents. I was so nervous because I had the letter in my bag. I waited until my father left for work to put it on his night stand.

The next morning I awakened to breakfast; my mom always made great breakfast when we came home. Over the meal she shared with me that my father had found the letter and had given it to her to read. She read the letter and commended me on being so honest and upfront. She also apologized for not being able to be there for me to talk over the issues I had been feeling. She reassured me that this was a great beginning to a new relationship with my father.

As I began to go up the stairs he was coming down. His face looked very somber and still. I backtracked and was standing close to the doorway. He had the letter in his hand. I was so shocked. Now what do I do I thought? I now had to confront everything I'd written in the letter, face to face!

When he got to the bottom of the stairs, we embraced each other and my dad said, "You know daddy loves you; you know daddy loves his little Ree!" ('Ree' is my nickname my dad gave me from one of my middle names 'Maria').

For the first time in a long time I found solace in his embrace. I felt like a little girl again being held by my daddy. The security I had once lost was now restored. I said, "Yes daddy, I know!" In that moment, years of pain, hurt, and rejection were healed. I was eternally grateful to God to now be free!

IN-TO-ME-SEE

I know for some people, you may be asking "Why didn't she just write the letter a long time ago?" It wasn't apparent to me until a year before, that these issues had an affect on who I was and had become; one of the subtleties in life I often omitted as 'no big deal.' Everybody has some pain, or it wouldn't be life, right? So in essence, we dismiss things that ultimately come back to haunt us in forms of questions or confrontations or even stages in life.

The "Lets talk" comment that came from my college boyfriend was his way of saying, 'IN-TO- ME- SEE' (intimacy). He wanted us to connect beyond the barrier; but because I had never been intimate with myself, I didn't know how to be intimate with him. I had so many barriers that he realized he was only going to get so far into who I was, and he wanted more.

The *more* was what I couldn't give; it was what I spent years pushing away and rejecting. It was what I feared the most. I didn't even know that is what he wanted until years later. I was haunted by the many questions I encountered thereafter, because I was unable to come up with a practical response, to an emotional engagement.

Intimacy is so important in discovering love. Every person has a longing to be intimate and have a deep connection. Most run in fear because they do not trust the acceptance that one is wishing to be granted in order to be given access behind the walls of our hearts.

We internalize our pain and end up rejecting the very thing God created us to have. How then do we experience the fullness of love if we ourselves are not free enough to pursue it? We over exert energy to systematically prevent ourselves from being the vessels God intended. We remain slaves to fear, that cripples our ability to pursue our purpose and destiny in life. Instead we settle for the casualties of our inner war and "hope" for the *best* that may never come. We accept haphazard, meaningless relationships as a means to soothe a craving for something more, something richer, and deeper.

The results are either we become numb and distant or we become angry and resentful. No matter our reaction, the core of our existence is still the desire to be loved and needed. We long for someone to fill the inner well, and ensure that we remain full. Nothing is more saddening than watching people who have never been healed from pain enter into relationships, only to feel alone and isolated. They gauge the eyes to their partner's soul to fulfill a yearning that was never created for them to fill. They force their partner to meet unrealistic expectations that only put a band-aid on their pain and suffering, never dealing with the root problem.

Sure, pain seems extreme looking at it for what it is. But I believe that is why we clothe it with other things, so that it remains covered and hidden. We avoid people who do not accept the mediocrity of ephemeral relationships, and pursue an endless circle of superficial realities that all together define our short-lived successes.

Discovering the *more* begins with allowing yourself to see yourself for who you are, with all your blemishes and insecurities, and taking a seat in the vehicle of self discovery; only to encounter what has come to make you who you are today.

Part Two

What is Love?

His Love ≤ My Love

Why is it so difficult to accept God's love? I find it so strange that it was 'so easy' for me to say or try to show God how much I loved him, but the reverse was ignored by my inner struggle to accept something I could not return. The vastness of His love is something that theologians and mankind have tried to figure out for all of our existence. The mere premise that God loved us first should, in essence be, enough, right? I am so mesmerized by the notion of love = love, meaning that because He loved me I can love Him. Only in my world, it was His Love ≤ My Love. That equation is both sad and well practiced.

Calvary alone was the greatest example of true love and dedication. It was by this demonstration I was cast away by the idea of who I truly was. I knew in myself that I didn't have the ability to love in that way. It seemed both unnatural and fitting to my current way of living to become so vulnerable that someone else's needs superseded my own, through laying down my own life.

You have to understand that this is not just dying for a close friend or family; this is dying for your persecutor, your enemy, and those who seek to devour your existence through heinous acts. What Christ did was unparallel to anyone's actions in my own life. So why did I find it so unsettling to nuzzle myself underneath His nail-scarred hands and rest in His love?

True acceptance of Christ can only come through revelation of one's lack thereof. I found it profound that I said I loved Him and yet rejected His love. Anyone on the outside could see the irony of this thought process, and yet the first mistake was trying to analyze something that was never meant to be comprehended. "No greater love has no man than this...[i] "For God so loved the world...[ii]" These verses speak to something more powerful than words can depict.

Some people believe 'The best things in life aren't free...' which suggests nothing good comes without a price. Only in this case it does. Christ paid the ultimate price so that I didn't have to and what I then get in return is something more than what I spend a lifetime trying to give back.

He Loves Me?

Kirk Franklin, current noted hip-hop gospel artist, wrote a song called, 'He Loves Me'. The lyrics are so real to me. 'He loves me even when I go against His will, He loves.... Jesus I am so grateful for your Love.'

As I listened to this song I would become overwhelmed, *only for a moment,* by the words. I am so focused on the 'go against His will' that I cannot even absorb the point of the song. I immediately begin repenting for things of which I have already been forgiven. I think about all the things I have done that have caused me to be separated and then go into my taunting cycle of telling God how much I love Him for being so gracious. Yet, I have missed the important part of the song. "HE LOVES ME!!"

I still do not resonate with the passion from whence this song was written. Because of His love, I am grateful not because of my forgiven sin; my sin is forgiven out of LOVE.

Why is it that when songs like these are played, I feel more condemned than I do overwhelmed with worship and praise? After all, it is His love that makes the difference. My sin will never cease; my flesh is forever flawed and I continue to try to work to love someone who just LOVES ME!

As this journey began to unfold in my life, I found that God was speaking to me in so many different ways. He was showing me in demonstration after demonstration who He was, and how my purpose was birthed out of His Love for me. It is in the midst of these manifestations where revelation comes to life and I am re-introduced to God.

Naturally Speaking

One of the ways God revealed himself to me was through nature. I felt a sense of closeness and security being in the midst of His creation. Those times of tranquility and reflection provided me with a deeper admiration for God that surpassed what I had come to know before.

I love going to the water! There is something so peaceful and calm about watching the water. In college, I spent a lot of time at Alki Beach in the southwest part of Seattle, Washington, going just before sunset to watch the changing of the day into night and admiring the atmosphere. It was always amazing to me how the water behaved. How can this mass phenomenon be so subtly controlled and non-threatening? The waves would rise up and then become small incoming puddles on the shore.

I would sit on a nice long log at a distance from other people near the water; away from the city noise and traffic of cars and people walking along the sidewalk. I sat in a place where the only distraction was the breeze that hit my face and the birds that flew back and forth. I sat alone.

Alki Beach was my place of escape, my place of serenity. I knew I could find God there. I am well aware of the omnipresence of God, but I felt connected to God in that place of solitude. To me, there was no one but God and me at Alki Beach. This was the place where my heart began to converse with His heart and we had a deep understanding, a deep connection. This was the place where I found refuge and strength. This was the place of communion, sweet communion in the midst of His creation!

I used to wonder what God was thinking when it was stated, *"Let the waters under the Heaven be gathered together unto one place, and let the dry land appear: and it was so. And God called the dry land Earth; and the gathering together of the waters called the Seas: and God saw that it was good."* iii

God had such an order and He was so specific in how He positioned everything. In the simplicity of His commands came a complex conception of God's mind. A special gift and example He provided of his spoken love. His divine dictation manufactured an existence from the dark and there I sat in the midst of it all, He and I alone.

I spent many nights at Alki Beach with God, just trying to decipher what my purpose was, and He intimately shared with me things that would only be revealed in time, and never repeated in mere words.

Sometimes I went to Alki to cry tears I didn't want anyone else to see. Other times I sat there and my heart said nothing as I inhaled the newness and exhaled the pain.

Naturally speaking, God was demonstrating His love and I was showing Him my faith. What made me believe that the water would never overtake me or that the log would sustain me? What made my faith in the creator and great architect so divine that I never questioned His craftiness and design? I was on a journey to know God, not the God I had known before, but the God of "More"... More of whom He was that I never knew before... More that beat against my heart like a drum with a yearning I had felt for years but was afraid to investigate. I wanted to know more about God!

As I sat out on that beach alone, it was my way of getting a sneak preview into the vastness of who He was without any fear or hesitation. That time for me was non-threatening and free.

Mountain High Valley Low

Being outdoors in the Pacific Northwest, the distant shadow of the mountains was so distinct that I could envision every sharp curve and slope; and in the same view I could see the valleys in between.

It amazed me how I would always see a valley before I saw another mountain. The revelation of seeing this pattern reminded me of my life journey. It was foretelling a future on which I was embarking. Where there is a mountain you will always see a valley.

It reminded me that even if I were in a valley, currently, there would always be a mountain on the horizon. I was on my way up! And whenever I *would* stand on top of that mountain, I *would* see the top of the next mountain; and so, I kept that in mind as I descended knowing that there *would* be another mountain in life that I *would* have to climb. Faith is revealed in hindsight.

> *"For every mountain you brought me over, for every trial you seen me through"* I imagined Jesus talking with his disciples saying to them, *"whoever says to this mountain..."*[iv]

Presently, in my imagination I can see Jesus pointing to the mountains that I see in my view here in Seattle. I, then look inward to see the mountains in my life with their sharp curves and slopes that are well-defined. Suddenly, yet poignantly, the sun of my tomorrow is seeping behind them as night finally comes.

I say to myself as little Annie said in her great stage production, *'The sun will come out tomorrow,"* and like David said in Psalms 30:5, "W*eeping may endure for a night but Joy comes in the morning"*

Darkness has come, yet as I look out among the water and the mountains I see the trees. The beauty of living in the Pacific Northwest is the outdoors, which is as gorgeous as it is productive to life: the nice tall trees are a sign of oxygen which provides air and life.

When I drive down the highways I see the trees; and when I look in the distance, I see the trees on the mountains. That tells me that even on the mountains there is life. I see life in the silhouettes of the mountains. As I look, I begin to think that some mountains aren't meant to be moved or removed; they are meant to be 'climbed over'

As I climb over what God has placed in my life, I realize I will not die as I go over each mountain, for each mountain is only but a moment in time. I can have confidence in this because those trees have been there for years and years. Their roots are so ingrained in the mountain that they are not going anywhere.

God loves me enough to already have trees in position on the mountain so that when it gets tough, and the higher I climb, even though it will be even harder to breath, I will live!

Being outside gives me a revelation and communication I do not receive from anywhere else. It is my time to commune with God in a special way. It is where I was introduced to the vastness of His existence. His creation majestically speaks for itself. I sit in the stillness of His presence, at peace with my surroundings because He is there. And it is in those moments I am reminded of my life journey and discovery, as He and I sit alone.

Uncovering the Truth

True Lies

It was evident each day that the more I remained in the same mental and emotional condition; I would die a slow death. The lies I fed my flesh everyday for nourishment were only poisoning the destiny being birthed on the inside of me. I had exhausted every ideology that I had known to be true and was at the point of passing out. What was it that I was searching for? What was it that created such a void in my life?

You see the lies I told myself were 'true lies', lies that at one time had some fashion of reality but over time seeped into imagery and became falsified by life's utter pleasures. The facade that I had to maintain in moments like this could have been overly suffocating, because of the lack of air that was supplied in darkness. The grimness of it all was that I never thought they were lies. I had convinced myself that the 'truthdom' that I lived by was foundational. All the more disguising were the barriers in my life with their overindulgence in an allegiance to pious living which only resulted in fear and lack of discipline.

The voids seemed to multiply as time went on; it felt like things weren't right. The foundation was becoming shaky and I was angry at God for not exposing me to what I felt was the truth.

What truth was I looking for? For me, the recognition that I had spent a lifetime trying to define the precise measurements of a nicely designed box for God to fit in was devastating. Instead of reaching for more, I would settle for just enough to get by. That is all I thought my religious works had become worth. 'A slip–n-slide' of dedication to something I could never obtain. The anger inside only increased with the frustration of knowing that the box I was building, I found myself also trapped in it. At this point it was a spiritual catastrophe, and I was unable to relieve myself of the trap I had so easily walked in.

Like most people, I could begin the blame game and start pointing fingers at everyone in the world around me. However, in this case I was the only one who would have to one day 'give an account' for me. It wasn't that I didn't live the 'saved' life and wasn't dedicated to serving God, but what did it all mean? I had reached a place in my life where I had climbed the mountain of self righteousness and there was no more top to surpass. All of the excitement behind the adventure had ceased and I was overwhelmed with disappointment that even my effort could be displeasing to God. "What more could He want?" I thought to myself. I really didn't want to do this anymore. I had decided that I was going to step away from everything I knew to be true and start over again.

I began to say if God were really who He said He was to me all my life, then He would show me who He was in a new way - a way that was not bound to a denomination or a personal motivation; a way that would make His word come to life for me. I was so spiritually dried up that tiny sips of living water only brought on intense thirst and hunger pains.

I was yearning for something beyond what I could comprehend; something that would sustain me even when I jumped off the treadmill and just wanted to walk naturally.

The one thing I knew for sure was that *GOD WAS REAL!* He was not a she or positive energy or some **being** aimlessly hovering in space. He was God: all knowing, all powerful, all encompassing GOD! But what that meant for me personally was another story.

GROWING PAINS

In a way, I wanted to start over. The pressure of the pedestal that the world had put me on was so much that I could not even take being awake some days. I just wanted to live my life. This must be how celebrities feel. Being in the spotlight all of the time was so draining and there was little room, if any, for error.

There were things in my life I was still learning and understanding about who I was. I didn't really know me. I wanted to know who Christal was and what made me 'tick.' What was I was supposed to be molded into? How did He intend for my life to go? Growing in the public eye was so difficult. Every mistake I made seemed like it was broadcast on the 'Church Folk *'you're a sinner* radio. I could never understand why people cared about what I did so much.

The more scrutiny I was put under, the more I realized that I, too, had once been like a Saul persecuting people for who they were instead of understanding or accepting them for who they were. No one took the time to even talk to me or listen to what I had to say. It was "here is the list of scriptures of which you are in direct violation." I wanted to 'puke' every time they used God's word to try to hurt me. I was like, "They cannot be serious!"

There I was trying to figure out life and all they could see were my mistakes. The funny thing was I knew God wasn't seeing my life the same way they were. I could no longer stomach the hypocrisy. Living for people became less and less tantalizing and "I don't care" became my new mantra! And at that point it was as if I was feeding their daily show with more and more news.

I became cynical and would give them information to talk about; at least they would know from the source. The same people that I prayed with, fasted with, and ministered with were the same ones that when I was going down off the mountain of 'Self Righteousness' were spiritually kicking me down further. They had no comprehension that they themselves were on a mountain top basking in a glory only built by man. At this point I guess you can say I was tumbling down, though there was a strange feeling of relief as I fell. I could feel my lungs filling up with air again and even as I was embarking on uncertainty, I still felt secure in knowing that I was no longer going to be trapped by my own reality.

It amazed me how quickly the world turned upside down. It seemed like a wild forest fire burning up everything in sight. I resented everything for which they stood. I had realized that what was meant to be a service to God became a circus for men. I was ashamed. How did I allow what at one time had been so pure in heart to become so convoluted with religious acts of worship that were not truly centered on God. Yes, the word of God was secure, but the premise by which I had evolved and the spiritual notion that I had allowed to be my existence was old and stale.

What fruit had I born in this existence? "They shall know you are My disciples by the fruit that you bear. "ᵛ Sure fruit was growing but what kind? Were they ripe or unripe when I picked them off? Was I even allowing God to prune the trees on which they grew?

I pondered where the turns occurred. What happened and where did the knots begin? Just trying to process that became too much for me. I knew that what I had encountered up to this very point in my life was not all in vain! I knew that the sincerity from which it was birthed still remained tucked away, hidden in my soul, just waiting to be rediscovered.

Like a prisoner, I wanted to be free. I didn't even think about what free really meant. How did I define free? It didn't matter at the time. All I could see were bars in front of the light. It makes no sense to have broken fetters but still be behind bars. I was walking around a cell living in my own sense of freedom but comfortable by the degree to which I could roam.

The bars defined the distance I could go: No farther than this point was what I told myself. In doing so, I was killing off anything that was trying to cause me to grow past my set limit. Starving myself, I was stunting my spiritual growth so that I would not out grow my cell. Yet at the same time, I was crying for freedom I could not define.

Wasn't I already free? I had no chains on me! So why should I complain about the bars? At least they were keeping me from danger unseen. But more and more that excuse did not hold weight and I wanted to see beyond my 'now.' What about my tomorrow?

Forcing myself to feel a conviction that did not come from God, I was stuck with the guilt from asking questions in that manner. Purpose was a word I used, and not a way of life. I had reached my plateau and peaked on the highest height of ....who really knows?

How long would I remain this way? I was confined to the prison within my mind, numbing my desires so that I couldn't feel my heartbeat anymore. I was so tired of running up against the same walls. I could see them coming but, yet, I ran directly towards them. Pretending as if this time they would not be there, my falsified hope had only turned to bitterness and rage.

In order to still feel like I had covered ground I would run laps in circles. These laps allowed me to convince myself that I was indeed going somewhere. Yes, I was going but only in the same direction to "NOWHERE"!

"Give us Free"

I was too 'by the book' to ever physically end up in a prison; however, being physically free and held captive in my mind was far worse. I was not taking hold of what I had available to me. What those who were physically locked up wouldn't give to be where I was; however, I was too self-minded to understand the freedom I already had.

Everyone knows when you use a lock you never swallow the keys, so that you can always be able to unlock the lock. It wasn't that I had swallowed the keys, I had so many I didn't know which keys went to which lock. It would take a life-time, I thought, to figure this out.

For it took a lifetime to get them to this point in the first place.

The agony of going in circles was ridiculous. I kept thinking *'get it together already!'* At least that is what I would have told any one of my friends in this situation. But taking my own advice would actually mean I would have to admit that something, somewhere, at some point went wrong. I was in no place to admit much of anything. I was still 'figuring' this entire existence out.

Even Luther Vandross could see, *'You got me going in circles...round and round and round and round...'* Did I intend to continue to find comfort in this mess? When would it all end? I would hate to die and be in the condition in which I was at this time. What would people say about me? I didn't want to think about it because there were so many ways that it could go. I was going nuts trying to break it all down.

I mean who thinks about their Eulogy in a time like this? The statues of pride I had built provided great shade from the scorching sun of reality. I wanted to be free, I really did, but, free from what; and to do what? What was it that I was going to do once I got free? I knew freedom was a gift and I did not want to have it lie dormant and unused. But I could not remember what it was like and how it would feel.

So I continued to let myself fall at a rapid pace, knowing once I reached the bottom, I then could be free. The fall was not short and quick, but long and hard. I was like 'man how high was I?'

It seemed like I was falling into a bottomless pit. Each lock I opened catapulted me farther down. I was rolling all over the place. "Down and down she goes, where she stops nobody knows!"

What I found so amazing about all of this was God provides us so much grace in times like these. There I was knocking myself down, destroying everything ever erected in my life only to start over without any purpose or plan. You would think that would be the end. All the while, I was still holding onto stuff that should have crumbled as I tumbled downward.

Unlocking the Locks

The keys to my heart were such a mystery. Because while my life had this unrealistic view of being free within bounds, my heart was suffering from the wear and tear of the various locks that kept it so secure. Some of the locks to my cell were things that I feel all of us in life have encountered: pride, pain, and a loss sense of self, insecurity, distrust, lack of direction, lack of purpose, and fear.

Recognizing these locks helped my journey progress beyond the place of misunderstanding and allowed my eyes to see in the midst of the fog. I had wrestled with these locks for too many years of my life. Unlocking these locks weren't the ultimate solution but it was a breakthrough to me taking another step in the right direction.

Until a person can recognize what things within themselves keeps them bound, s/he will never be able to embark on a journey of discovery with any real meaning. Sure people do self-searches all the time, finding their inner peace and solitude, trying to be happy with the restrictions that they have put on themselves as a means to move forward, only to find they are taking larger steps backwards in return.

It is easy to want to do minimal work and desire enormous results! However, I find that the easiest principle to follow, working toward something is only beneficial if you see instant results. So anything that requires endurance or long suffering must not be meant to be.

It is under these pretenses that many of us find ourselves short of ever uncovering truth in our lives. The words my life spoke were just that very thing. This wasn't happening the way I wanted it to happen or going at the pace I thought it should go, so maybe I was just wasting time focusing on something that wasn't really my problem.

Pride

I could write about *pride* for a lifetime. Pride is the greatest purpose killer ever known. It is one of the things God detests, because it causes us to be frozen and stiff - unable to see past ourselves and discover our future.

If all we can see is ourselves and our immediate superficial needs, how is it possible to truly assess the reality of our life?

It was so difficult for me to admit where I really was. It wasn't until I had already begun to fall that I started contemplating what was happening. I didn't want to come to grips with the truth that I was the sole cause of this circumstance I found myself in. I mean, I was Christal Jenkins, this young exuberant, educated, well-versed, accomplished woman with so much ahead of me. How could someone like me be in the midst of all of this? Impossible if you ask me. "It isn't as bad as it seems! This will all go away and I will not have to let anyone know the truth." After all they came to me for advice and support. So, how can those who leaned on me be strong enough for me to lean on them? "I am strong enough to endure this and therefore I can take on my life and the lives of others. What doesn't kill me will only make me stronger, right?"

My disease of pride was eating away at my brain everyday, and it was manifesting like an in-grown tumor.

My lies fed it and fed it and fed it until it was so large it was growing on the outside as well.

My pride put me on the fast track of failure. "What would people think of me if I told them what I was dealing with? No one would want to talk to me about their issues because they would think that I was incapable of providing them with anything worthwhile since I couldn't even apply my own advice."

This uneasiness caused me to become even more stubborn and closed. I didn't want to hear what anyone really thought about what was going on. Sure people would ask and I would tell them I was doing fine, which I was because I had convinced myself I was normal and I just had to deal with it and get over it. All in all I was screaming on the inside for someone to see past my facade and come rescue me.

What began to unlock the lock was finally admitting that I was dying on the inside. If God didn't help me I might never recover.

It is funny how we wait until everything is about to fall to hell, then want a savior, when all we had to do was just acknowledge our need in the beginning. We can prevent a majority of the consequences to which we become subjected because of our pride.

I could never understand how I could ignorantly live my life knowing that it was messed up, just to protect something that was soon going to die. We all know that you cannot deny the stench of death. That smell is very distinctive and will only intensify until that which is dead is discarded.

Pain

I realized that pretending that life's events didn't bother me didn't mean that they will not bother me. A person can only absorb so much pain, depending on the impact of each blow; a few words can go a long way, one experience can cripple a lifetime.

I spent a good portion of my life playing make-believe: '*sticks and stones will break my bones but words will never hurt me.*' I was kidding myself to believe that I had somehow gained a super power that made me more superior than the entire human race.

I had acted as if nothing anyone did could affect me. Enduring so much pain had only made me numb to life. I lacked the luster that God created mankind to posses, for I had bought into a mentality that had no "Satisfaction Guaranteed!" policy.

Why is it more popular to be callus than to be pliable? Why is it okay to have pride in being numb and not in being real with your emotions?

I used to think that with life comes hail and rain; so build a larger fort! Okay, I know that sounded weird but I hope that you know what I mean.

All kinds of things are encountered in life, some good, bad and indifferent. The true recognition comes not in allowing everything to be a 'pity party' but an acknowledgement of your humanity.

We were never built to be life's punching bag or dumping ground. Allowing pain to sow seeds and be rooted in our lives can destroy us.

I continued to act as if 'what you say bounces off me and sticks to you!' When that just isn't true!

I have encountered things in my life like many of you that are very painful, and I have held onto them only so that people would not see the aftermath. I was afraid that people would take advantage of me if they saw one glimpse of weakness.

If superheroes were real, we would not be spending $30 to go to the movies just to watch their sagas unfold! We would be looking at each other! It is safe to say that the question remains, and even if I were to acknowledge it, then what? Some things are so painful they can cause us to experience true detriment by even the memory thereafter.

Until pain is exposed healing can never begin. I had to allow the old bandages to come off before I could even clean the wound. There were some things in my life that I could have easily glanced over because after all I had lived with it for this long, why even rock the boat!?

The decision to pursue life more abundantly instead of life based on survival, seemed more of a yearned pursuit. I didn't want to just get by; I wanted to experience a fullness I had never known. I didn't want to take this baggage with me because taking it would be like dumping my garbage into my suitcase and taking it with me on a nice tropical vacation. I would not be able to go to the beach without people noticing the smell. No matter what I thought, people could always see the residue of pain.

Pain screams louder than our voices can. I realized I did not have to carry this pain around for the rest of my life. I did not have to be heavy and burdened forever.

Unlocking the pain allowed me to be okay with my humanity and begin the process of wholeness from within.

Loss Sense of Self

Who was I? I found myself lost among the list of expectations people had placed on me. Living up to what others wanted disallowed me ever to define me!

What did I stand for and what did I believe? I lived incarcerated to people's ideas of who I was. Not wanting to ever disappoint the masses, I remained discontented and alone. A loss sense of self allowed for me to be isolated because I could make no direct connection with anyone. I was always living in a bubble that only allowed me to breathe the oxygen I was fed.

I had lost who I was; somehow it seemed as though I woke up and was having to perform great feats to remain alive. I didn't know how to cut the 'Pinocchio strings' to become a real girl.

I was choking on the laundry list of do's and don'ts; "sure I can do that"; "yes, anything else you need?"; "oh yes I will be praying for you,"; "of course I can come early to help, no problem!" "If you can't follow through on what you promised,"etc.

It is devastating giving and giving and giving to others only to never receive exactly what you are giving in return. Why was I continuing to subject myself to this over and over and over again?

What about my needs? What did I really want? The sad thing was that I didn't even know. I was so busy and caught up in what others needed and their expectations, I let myself go far off into the dark, to the back of my mind. I could hear short breaths at times so I knew I was still alive but where was I?

It was apparent to me that much of my deliberate decision to fall off course was a cry to discover myself. I wanted to know me! What that meant I still didn't know! Nonetheless, I wanted an understanding of who I was, and come to know what God had made so *"good"* in the beginning.

Now the only person at fault for losing myself was me, especially since I found myself lost in People, and not in God. By doing so, I remained lost and alone without being aware of my true purpose.

Losing yourself in a relationship, job, service or anything else is a sign that you want acceptance and assurance that validates your existence. You then become known by what you do and not by who you are. Since you don't even know who you are it works out for a while. But even the most vigilant workers find themselves burnt-out and wanting to embark on discoveries for themselves.

The truth that I found was in my mind; I knew this was true because when I felt taken advantage of I would list all the things I had done for that person. Why was I keeping track? I had created my own "Hall of Fame". If I were doing things for recognition only to prove self worth I would only be as great as my last deed.

After a while my measuring stick just seemed too small. I knew I had to be worth more than what I was contributing to the world.

Unlocking 'Loss of Self' allowed me to begin to discern my self worth and seek out who I was created to be!

Insecurity

As I told you before, my lack of security goes way back to when I was a child. I had struggled with feeling secure in myself because the security I had come to known was stripped away and I felt emotionally naked and exposed.

Without a strong sense of security I found myself searching for validation from places that always seemed to disappoint me. Why, you might ask? Because voids like this can only be filled with knowing who and whose you are. Knowing this creates an appropriate sense of belonging and pride, that births confidence and purpose within.

Without this awareness, you can feel like you are uncovered and exposed to whatever the world throws in your direction. At some point in your life, someone or something uncovered you. Being uncovered is dangerous because you feel trapped and confused about what you did to deserve what happened. No matter what occurred, you will live your life in light of the shame that stains your memory. It is like a broken record that continues to repeat the same three lines.

I believe that everyone in life has had a situation that made him/her feel insecure. This situation, no doubt, opened the door to more self doubt, disappointment and/or self hate. Your value was questioned and all you wanted was for someone to notice the cries from within.

Could anyone see the tears your heart cried? Could anyone hear the screams?

I wrestled with my security as a result of many situations in my life. They seemed to stack like building blocks and each layer was filled with painful memories.

I didn't know at the time, that all of the insecurities I had were all based out of the experiences I had encountered. I used my insecurities as motivation to prove to the world who I could be. I figured maybe then someone would notice me. The way I acted in relationships, toward family and friends, even my outlook on life were all molded by my lack of security.

Unlocking these insecurities opened the door for me to safely become uncovered again so that I could seek a true covering and find rest in a security that could be life sustaining.

Distrust

Why is it that everyone has issues with trust? I look at my godchildren and I see their innocence and how their little minds navigate through life. I am amazed how open and willing they are to trust people, yet they also have a keen sense of discernment to decipher when not to trust.

At what point in life did I stop trusting people? Why do I only trust people as "far as I can throw them?" which isn't very far!

We put people on trial at every moment waiting to accuse them of being disloyal and untrustworthy. We expect people to leave us with broken promises and disappointments. After all our dad or mom did it, our teacher or pastor did it, even our best friend did it; so what makes anyone else any different?

I found myself always keeping people away; I couldn't trust them to make me feel safe. I was afraid of what would happen if I let them in. What if they saw something they didn't like and rejected me for it? What if I opened up to them and they run off to tell everybody? What if I counted on them to be there and they did not follow through?

I have been let down, discouraged, and frustrated by my life experiences with people. I never thought mankind could be so cruel and abusive. But what I found was that the same people, who treated me like that, were hurting themselves from the same issues.

It is our natural tendency to project our feelings onto others. It soothes our misery and allows for us to detach ourselves from the pain in our own lives.

Lack of trust stems from so many of the other locks I have described. Unlocking this lock is allowing other locks to be exposed. In some ways distrust is merely a cover-up for other issues in our lives. It is our way of protecting ourselves from the arrows that try to pierce our souls.

I have found that being free to trust others started with me being able to trust myself. I had to first understand the root of my distrust which at times was like opening up the mysteries to Pandora's Box.

Lack of Direction/ Purpose

I have heard all my life, Jeremiah 29:11: "*For I know the plans I have for you, plans to prosper you, plans to give you a hope and a future.*"

My problem was not so much with God's plans; it was that God's plans didn't look like mine. I was constantly driving on the highway of life with no map or 'GPS' (Global Positioning System). Going straight when I should have turned; turning left when I should have turned right; running out of gas thinking I had a few more miles left in the tank!

I had dreams, goals, plans that I believed could have only come from God. The issue wasn't with the dreams or the plans, it was with the fact that I missed the point about "*a man's heart plans his ways and it is God who directs his step*" *(Proverbs 16:9)*. While embarking on this new journey to allow God to show me a new way of life, I had become lost trying to find my own way.

I was worried that I was missing opportunities and afraid of closed doors. I wanted God to bless my plans and make them work like He was a magician with a spell or a genie in a bottle. God's ability to go above and beyond what I had planned wasn't even comprehensible to me. I knew He had plans but so did I. I was so stirred and excited about what I could achieve. I was motivated that I was on the right track with how I saw my life.

The sad reality was that my view of life was so small in retrospect to God's and I was only limiting my potential and worth. Purpose is where destiny and eternity meet. My destiny was what God had written out before I was born; and eternity was God's unlimited ability and existence beyond life as I know it right now. Altogether, *purpose* provides direction. It is my spiritual 'Garmin' or 'Tom Tom'. It is what I can walk out each day of my life in faith knowing that God is guiding every step.

One might ask why is it that people are so afraid to let God be in the driver's seat. I am not sure if it is really that people are so much afraid as I think we are assured that we are doing him a service by putting him in the passenger seat while we drive, as if it is more important to us to see God take a break.

For me, I love to be in control of my life; that way I can safeguard any surprises or any extra sacrifices that would require a lot of responsibility. If I 'spoon-feed' myself my plans, then I can pace myself as I please, never having to be on any time clock but that of my own.

Unlocking this lock exposed the truth that my life was going everywhere but anywhere. The path I was driving on was only getting me so far and I could never unlock the potential to more.

Fear

Along with *pride,* I found that *fear* was another crippling effect. Fear allowed me to tell myself the lies I wanted to hear so that I could soothe myself through life, always avoiding reality. Fear caused me to focus on people and life and not on anything else. I became a slave to it and like the character Linus from 'Charlie Brown,' I held onto it like a comfort blanket. I dragged it along wherever I went. It became my pal and friend; I couldn't go to sleep without it.

Fear became my daily nourishment; it had great vitamins such as worry, defeat and stress which could lead to various physical elements that no one ever wanted to attribute to *fear.*

Why does *fear* have so much power? Why do we hide behind something so superficially secured? Everyone does it, but why?

I go crazy trying to figure out why it is more popular to walk in fear than it is to attempt to press toward victory.

For me my greatest fear was being successful. What would people think about me? They might think I was trying to be better than everybody! What if I get the position and he doesn't? What if my idea worked and theirs didn't? I wasted years of my life being crippled by fear - afraid to try to discover who I was in order to unlock my greatest potential in life.

Success meant always worrying about what people thought of me, what 'label' I had and how I could ease into things unnoticed. Just plain being successful seemed too leery for me. What if I attempted to achieve success only to fall short and have to try again? People would look at me as a failure. Yet, I knew that the worse thing a person could do was not ever try. It would be better to spend your life trying and never succeed then to have died never trying at all or quitting after the first try.

Fear spews lies that only destroy your inner being. It builds houses and settles inside your heart. It enables you to be mediocre, always settling for what you can get and nothing more. Your expectations become so low that you think you are excelling when you reach one feat above your base. Rising higher seems impossible. You begin to idolize people you see on TV or people you know who are successful and you worship them from afar. You never once see yourselves successful like them.

In unlocking my fear, I had to realize that my discovery of true love would be my only savior helping me shed the locks from my cell and move forward to finding out what truly was within.

Part Three

Back to the Basics

Starting Over

Starting over is something that looks differently for everyone. I had decided to just be... Be what? ...Still.

I didn't want to do anything as a means to allow God to do everything. I didn't want to pray, read, or do anything. I allowed my mind to be the blank canvas for the greatest artist this world had ever known.

My canvas loomed large enough for infinite possibilities with His creativity in abundance and exuding the potential for a divine masterpiece. I became clay so that I could be molded - shaped into something that He could use. Not knowing exactly what I was searching for, I knew the road led to Him. I had hoped that the road would lead to something beyond my greatest imagination, someplace I could only dream of; someplace where only I would never have to worry about waking up. This would be real. This would be something I could touch and taste; something that allowed every one of my senses to be stimulated.

I was motivated to walk out of the cell and to move toward the light I had only seen in the distance. Heading towards the unknown, all I could see was what was in front of me. I didn't even want to look back to see whether I had left anything behind; I only wanted to press forward.

Convinced this would be the last time I would have to begin again, I was ready, but ready for what? I didn't know what, but it was anticipating the unknown that made the discovery something I longed for. My soul yearned to grab hold of what it had been desperately in search of - the inevitable.

In my stillness, I did absolutely nothing. I just sat. I had to make sure I found what I was looking for this time. So, no more false starts or rewinds, I was going to get what I needed. I was in pursuit of something more. I simply refused to settle for anything less.

Determined to reach the goal that was set before me, I was going to stop at nothing to achieve it. I had gotten what I had asked for as I began to unlock each lock. I could hear the ping of the metal as it bounced off the ground, finally landing some feet away; each sound, a reminder of where I had been, never to repeat or return.

I could hear *purpose* calling my name and I wanted to answer, "Yes, I am here". I wanted to climb up the new mountain with destiny in tow as His grace went before me; I knew I would be safe. I wanted to set out to prove that my existence was not in vain. I had purpose in replace of my shame. I was going to reach for what I could not see and take hold of what I was given - a second chance to discover who God was, a chance to finally see what I had been missing, the piece that I tried to create on my own, and the one I tried to replace.

I was grateful for my new beginning, and I really meant it this time. I was in search of a treasure and I knew that the "X" marked the spot. It was the mark that Paul spoke of when he said, "*Forgetting those things which are behind me and pressing on to what is ahead.*"[vi] He spoke to "*I press toward the mark for the prize of the high calling of Jesus Christ.*"[vii] He, too, was in search of that which he did not see, but that which his soul knew was in front of him.

My discovery began like the lifecycle of a butterfly, my belly scraping the ground as I finally nestled in my resting place only to be engulfed by a cocoon that would nurture my transformation. Soon I would become a natural mystery, a beautiful flawless creation; something that was to be marveled and appreciated. God breathed and designed.

Finally, I would become "Me".

The Onion

Days and days turned into weeks, and weeks turned into months, and months turned into years in search of something deeper. Digging what began as a small hole was now a huge pit, and yet no answers had surfaced. I continued to go deeper, surpassing what I had previously experienced. Covered in dirt, I, without restitution, continued to plunge deeper and deeper!

I knew I would hit something soon; I had come way too far to even look up to see how to get out. As I dug deeper, I began to talk to God. It was not a prayer as some may understand; my talk with God was just a simple conversation. I wanted Him to get to know me.

God and I would talk and each time was deeper than the time before and much different than the communion He and I had years before. My heart said words; my soul was reassured. Strangely enough I felt closer to God by not using the tools I had once used to work for His acceptance. I had previously convinced myself that if I prayed harder, fasted longer and read every scripture, I could find solace in knowing He would accept me more.

The layers were being peeled away as I was being stripped of my old mentality in which I was so deeply rooted I was like an onion - each layer revealing more and more. As I got deeper to the core I found that I could barely stand to hold my old mentality. Like with an onion, my eyes were watery by the process, but I kept taking breaks just so that I could continue to peel away the layers.

Being still is difficult. Over time I found myself getting antsy and wanting to retreat to my old way. My heart said, "No!" I pressed on, layer by layer bearing a special type of pain. I was under the impression that by allowing the layers to be peeled away I was somehow showing God how much I loved him, when in actuality, it was His way of getting to the core so that He could show me His love unconditionally, without any hindrances in the way.

Layer upon layer it seemed like it never had an end. Each strip was like ripping the band aids off of an open wound. As anxious as I was to get to the end, I was stopped by the notion that He and I had only begun to touch the surface. Years and years of things that were tucked away were carefully removed through His divine sovereignty and grace.

Why His sovereignty? This was a process that required submission and a willingness to say "Yes" in spite of the cost so that He could take control. I know for some of you that did not sit well. The words *'submission'* and *'control'* are like clanging symbols or a submarine sinking to the bottom of your stomach. I, too, felt the same way. Those words pierced my core and I rejected everything for which they stood, I didn't want to be weak or taken advantage of; I was strong and could stand on my own.

So, I fought a fight that I had to win. He never forced me to surrender: His patience was beyond what I could comprehend. He just waited while watching me throw blow after blow, swing after swing, and kick after kick. What was I fighting exactly? By no means was I trying to fight God; I knew I wasn't trying to have a limp like Jacob. I was fighting my own will.

The Fight

Like a spectator at a fight, He watched on as the bell rang and 'Round One' was shown.

'My Will' and I were released from our corners. It was the fight of the century and would be a fight to the finish. Who would come out a champion? I had fought 'My Will' many times and lost. Being the underdog provided a sense of motivation but it also provided a sense of fear. I knew this fight would be intense. No one person wanted to surrender their will very easily; the ultimate challenge was the 'Spirit'" vs. 'The Flesh.'

He had the best seats in the house - right up front. I refused to give up this time! Wounded and bruised, I kept getting up. Stumbling at times, dodging blow after blow, I managed to survive each round. Hearing the bell ring was like music to my ears. I quickly returned to my corner, my heart and soul coaching me on my next move, strategically plotting my attacks that would lead me to victory.

The next round approached. I slicked myself down from head to toe, bound my gloves tightly to my wrists, and properly taped my ankles. I was ready to go back into battle.

I know you may be asking why was she fighting this fight alone? This was a fight I fought every day alone. Like many of you we wrestle against our will, always trying to do what we feel is right only to be overtaken in our moment of weakness. I had to fight this inner battle so that I could be able to allow Him to continue to peel away at me. The deeper the depth, the harder the fight; I was determined to win.

Even in the Garden Jesus being the Son of God had a match with His will. He knew He had to surrender and He knew His decision would be the ultimate fulfillment of purpose. Immersed in tears and heaviness, He cried out "... Not my will but Thine will be done."[viii]

Those words He spoke were so powerful and profound! Christ in the prime of His life having to battle one last time.

I, too, was going to have to die and my flesh would not give up without a fight. I wanted to be able to say those words. I wanted to be able to cry out from the inside, "Not my will but Your will be done!"

Jesus wasn't forced to say those words. But it came from a desire to see *'the more'* glorified. He knew there was more to His Father's creation than what they had experienced. He was the divine connection to *'the more'*, the pathway that provided direct access to the very existence humans had tried to create on their own.

Jesus, too, in the darkest moment of His life surrendered, to uncover what the world had yet to know. This very act was the reason I can now fight my own fight and discover what lies beyond my present way of life, to a new life where my heart can call *'Home.'*

Broken

Being broken was an experience I had never felt before; something that every person should encounter. It is through brokenness that life takes on new meaning. Broken, was the ultimate prize for winning the fight against 'My Will.'

After exhausting myself in a daily battle against 'My Will,' I received the title as 'champion' and then my act to surrender didn't come with a smile and a pat on the back, or a celebration. I found that in the process of being stripped from what I had known, I had been broken. I was uncovered and exposed not to be humiliated or abused but to be renewed. I had been broken - humbled before the cross that once was the scene where Christ himself was broken, a reminder of God's grace and yet a definitive monument for purpose. *"For it was by grace I had been saved through faith."*[ix] This grace allowed for who I was to be broken into pieces, only to be restored as a new creation. What new creation? I didn't really know, but anything was better than what I had been.

The mistake that I made and that many of us make is that we want to experience the fullness of who He is without having to lose ourselves. Yes, Salvation is free, but the will to live it and have a true experience comes with an undying sacrifice of oneself. Broken is a pain that I cannot describe, yet it is a peace that flows on the inside. I rested in knowing that I, too, will be changed. Like that butterfly in the cocoon, I was being transformed, shedding away old skin.

Where I presently existed was a place I entered into alone. No one was there but God and me. Consecrated, I remained still, broken into pieces that I could not put back together. Each piece was purposely misshaped so that they could never fit together the same.

Even in this existence, I was trying to take the 'Humpty Dumpty' approach. You know *"Humpty Dumpty sat on a wall, Humpty Dumpty had a great fall, all the kings horses and all the kings men couldn't put Humpty together again."* I tried to use my surroundings as a crutch, hoping that my environment could put me back together again. Hence, I missed the entire reason I was in this place to begin with. This is what I wanted, right? I wanted to discover more. Usually, there is not much conversation about being broken. People don't like to tell others about their brokenness. I feel this is for a couple reasons.

First, many people have never allowed God to break them, so they cannot talk about something they have never experienced. Secondly, it is not a topic that excites people. No one wants to hear about having to die to themselves only to surrender their will to be broken down, reconstructed, molded and made into greatness. Sure most people want to be great but they all seem to want the, *"Here are 10 steps to be great in God"* or *"Here are the 7 principles to ..."* No one seems to embark on a discovery in which the only certainty is that they will never be the same. We all have to realize that this journey has no time limit; it is not wrapped in 12 steps. This journey begins and ends in eternity.

If I had known earlier in life what I later learned, my perspective would have been much different. I spent many nights frustrated with everything I was experiencing. I wasn't sure if I was headed in the right direction, and I tried to find answers in places that came up short of what I needed. I was afraid of what I did not know. But yet there was still a curiosity within that drove me to stay the course even when I wanted to quit. The further I went the more intense it became. It seemed like I was a moving target. Everything that could hit me tried, and some were right on target.

To be broken is sacred and solemn. Being broken was where I truly 'faced the music.' No more excuses, no more distractions, no more back peddling, it was just God and me. He was chipping away at me and I was still. He was cutting away at me and I was still. He was peeling away at me and I was - you guessed it - *still*.

Sure I moved occasionally, thinking I could support God in his efforts as if my assistance would speed up the process. Even though it seemed like I was merely adding time, another discovery of a layer that I needed peeled away.

It was in this place that my heart was being drawn closer to God, and I knew I was getting warmer. I wanted so badly to have what I had yet to possess. Therefore, I remained steadfast to a process and a journey in my place of solitude, in the midst of His blueprint, I sat broken and still.

Being Molded

The Clay

Throughout my life, I had heard of the example of the 'Potter and the Clay.' Even as a young child, I would be a 'potter' with play dough when playing with my siblings. The result was more fun than the process but it was all worth it. What was interesting to me about the way the story of the 'Potter and Clay' was taught, no one ever spoke from the point of what it took to make the clay. It was just shared in regards to the clay being molded and shaped.

I wondered what ingredients the Potter used when creating the clay. After all, it wasn't just sitting there, as well as, it had no existence without preparation.

The clay symbolizes you and me. I wonder what ingredients God uses when He desires to create purpose?

Clay is a composite of specific elements that once put together, properly provides a pliable solution that one can use at one's discretion. Each element is carefully measured and added in a specific order so as not to disrupt the texture of the substance. It has to come together just right in order for it to serve its true purpose. The process is carefully planned out so that it leaves time for the next steps. Nothing is rushed; taken into consideration is knowing this is not the end but a means to creating the masterpiece that is so vivid in the potter's mind.

Being broken provided me the experience of becoming clay. I had to be stripped down and specific characteristics had to be added. I was carefully mixed together in *love* to become a substance He could use to shape and mold as He pleased.

The Potter

God put vision and thought into what He foreknew - that which He had envisioned while He was completing His preparation. He eagerly awaited the opportunity to mold and make something out of the substance He had already created. You see, it is not as if the 'Potter' was making something out of nothing. He was aware that it took something to make it what it was, but for it to become what He had designed, it would need to be transformed.

Imagine the thoughts of the Potter. He already has set in His heart how He will mold each mound of Clay. Carefully placing it on the armature, He begins. His hands become positioned perfectly with the right firmness so as not to provide too much pressure, just enough to allow Him to mold to the level of detail He desires. His hands continue in a specific motion. He is almost systematic in His approach, yet He is careful not to mold this one like the others.

Keeping His eyes on the texture of the Clay as it is molded; He makes sure it does not dry out. The Clay remains well covered and provides living water to ensure that it will remain pliable. Without water, the Clay will crack and crumble into pieces preventing it from being used at all.

The Potter is well aware of the future targets He has set in His heart for this special Clay. He continues to work knowing that what was once a concept conceived in His mind, was now coming to life and purpose, taking shape as He intended.

The Fire

The fire allows for what was molded to be firmed and made solid. It must be set at a specific temperature so that the clay won't burn or ever harden.

Nothing can prepare you for the fire. The fire is not like being broken in that you do not have to be stripped and prodded. You are simply having your compositional makeup put through rigorous conditions to make certain it will stand; to ensure that it will be able to serve the purpose it was created for.

My fire was intense. After being shaped and molded I was put into the fire. I knew that everything that had been placed within me was now being tested. I was on my way to discovering the newness I had craved. I was becoming the woman that He wanted.

The fire tested what I was really made of; I couldn't sneak away from this process. All Clay if it had an immediate purpose must be put through the fire before it can be used. This is why it was even more important that I remain full of living water, moist enough to be molded so that the moisture I had absorbed would allow for me to be protected against the heat I was going to have to endure.

Life as I knew it had changed. I was experiencing things I never dreamed possible. Life was hot and very uncomfortable. Being in the fire was dark and all I could feel was the heat on all sides. What was not peeled away in me was being burnt away - seared and dissolved into ashes that would forever be un-recoverable.

I was in the fire, the place in which God intended His creation to go.

The process of being molded and going through the fire was reflective of how my life would rotate in regular order with each new level in God. This was not a one time experience.

This is how you determine if the Clay was made properly or not. This is why I had to remain still in the process of being broken, not forcing God's hand but being led by it. It was important that I remain open so that nothing was left untouched. I had to make sure that enough of the layers were peeled back in such a way that I had just the right foundation for the characteristics and likeness to be placed within me.

Eternity is a hard stick to measure against. Most people find it too difficult to comprehend. I find it to be a great mystery, and something that even after I die will only experience and never have a definitive definition.

Seasons in our life are so strategic. God knows when they begin and when they change. That is why I said it is important to yield to His sovereignty. In most cases, I really didn't know what lay ahead and I came to realize it was best if I didn't know, the better off I was. Otherwise I, like most people, would have found creative ways to cut corners. I would have been trying to develop shortcuts as a means to an end but still wanting to reap all the benefits and results, overlooking the benefits that lie within the process itself.

Being transformed was a blessing in disguise. It was something that I could not take for granted. It was through this process that I grew one step closer to discovering more and more of what it was I'd set out to find in the beginning. It was by this process I could share with others. I can truly say that I have been made new. It was by this process that God's ultimate plan was fulfilled. After all, could Jesus have risen if He never died? If He had never suffered on the cross, then He would never have been tormented to death. 'The process' was portrayed by God's greatest act of love.

It was through the fire that I began to discover what I was searching for; I could not conjure up myself. It was something that I needed to accept and come to know. As more and more of me was being burned away, I began to awaken to realize that what I had given up before was not a true sacrifice. It was only by mere experience that I received this revelation. All my life, I had avoided the very process that would provide me the fulfillment I was looking for.

As my flesh died an intense death, it was there in my purest moment that I saw one thing, one thing that was very clear, something I had never seen before. *God's heart!*

Open the eyes of my heart

Reflection

I was taken aback, and amazed by the image I saw in front of my face. Each pulse was an image of mankind beating vibrantly with a flow so fluid that it only spewed out an abundance of life. With His heart pumping rapidly as I drew close I was compelled to look deeper and so I did. Seeing something so vividly, it was as if my eyes and mind were playing tricks on each other. I stared harder trying to make out the image that was only getting larger as I moved closer. His heart's reflection had a familiar silhouette and my eyes were canvassing over to decipher what was in my view. Each beat was becoming louder and louder. I was so drawn to what was in front of me, drawn to something few people see and are eager to get close enough to touch Him. Staring into his heart, the image was no longer a blur; it no longer hid among the shadows. It was crisp and precise. I was moved with tears because now I was face to face with His heart.

The reflection was more moving than my own position, because for the first time I had uncovered a secret that was never meant to be kept unknown; He had provided me clues - signs that would lead me to the very discovery I was trying to find. As I looked on, the reflection I saw in His heart was mine!

Overwhelmed by this reality, I felt a sense of guilt. What His heart reflected about who I was, showed me the impeccable love and adoration God had for His creation. I felt guilty, why? Because all these years I had spent my time doing things I felt would make me become accepted and loved and all in all, His heart beat had never changed. His love for me was the same.

I saw Christal, the little girl, standing in the aisle with the tear down her face. I saw Christal, the young teen, ministering to other youth. I saw Christal with the knife pressed tightly to her chest; I saw Christal the college student, running off her frustrations. I saw me - Christal - at the water in the midst of His presence. I finally saw Christal standing face to reflection. The almond shape of my eyes, the button nose, the plump limps, I saw the details of my life in my own reflection.

His heart beat for me like a Timpani drum in a symphony; it was His longing I felt that had drawn me to discover more. It was His love my heart yearned to explore. All my life I was on a journey just to discover His love. I silently wept. It was the first time that it was God and me alone, intimately looking into each other's hearts. It was the first time I was not afraid to be open before Him. I laid my head against His heart and cried.

I had spent a lifetime showing Him how much I thought I loved Him, and never let Him show me. I wanted Him to count the ways and He wanted me to count the ways, also.

In the midst of something so powerful and unconditional, it made everything I had ever done before *vain*. Why vain? Because my adoration and worship was only reciprocating that which I would allow myself to experience; I was closed to God's love out of ignorance and lack of acceptance and I was unwilling to take the journey alone. And so I tried to give Him something that He never gave to me – or so I thought!

His love became more potent than the strongest elixir. I became undone. I was transfixed, in a trance, taken over by a 'toxic aroma.' It was something so distinctive and sweet I could feel the gentle chills moving throughout my body. I felt so tranquil, so at peace. I knew that I never wanted to leave, and this time I knew that I would never have to leave.

My state of being was more than a picture I could paint, more than a book I could ever write, more than a song, I could ever sing. It was more than I imagined in my deepest REM sleep. It was more than my wildest day dream, more than a sensual caress, it was just *more*.

I melted, like my first crush, in His arms. I was so giddy and excited by this understanding; I was in the arms of eternity, never ending and infinite. I stayed and remained still.

Our spiritual exchange emulated more than mere words could ever communicate. It was as if it made even His dreams come true. It was what He had longed for since He breathed life into His creation and it was what my heart panted for like a 'deer pants for the water'.

I knew, and He knew, and He knew, and I knew, that I was His and He was mine. We were never to be separated by life's utter strife. We were two peas in a pod, in love, and in a love that satisfied the depth of my soul. I was no longer crying to be free; I was captivated by His existence in me.

Our exchange resonated with the true definition of worship; our non-verbal rang out loudly, and our communion was sweeter than a honey comb.

I knew now that I was in love. Why? Because for the first time I truly loved someone more than I loved myself. I disappeared, and His reflection was all that I saw in my heart. He owned every space, I didn't care what He would find because I knew I was His and He was mine.

His love was like a drizzle of rain coming over me; I lifted my head ever so slightly to see that even God cried.

He and I in our most vulnerable states of being, lacked a peripheral vision to see anything outside of each other.

Now I could inhale the newness and exhale greatness. I no longer released any pain. There were no expectations - just enjoyment in a moment that would last for eternity.

My imperfection wrapped so tightly in His perfection made me perfect in time.

Infinite possibilities of what our relationship could become, therefore, I looked with hope into my future.

I now understood when it was said, "Now abides these three things –faith, hope and love and the greatest of these is *love*."[x]

"He Loves Me This I Now Know"

I could finally relate to the song "Jesus loves me this I know" only it wasn't just the Bible that told me so, but He Himself.

My heart knew it to be true, and there was nothing anyone could do to change that. I was determined to reciprocate everything I received which remained a continuous exchange of love that would continue even beyond death: 'Til to death do us part' wasn't a part of our covenant vows.

Ours was a love story that He and I would write together; I was the paper as He held the pen. Each stroke stylistically illustrated my purpose and each line became a testament to greatness wrapped in His divinity.

Carefully taking His time to make sure every page conveyed the meaning He intended, it was a book no one could put down.

I was in love with someone who made me happy, someone who made me free. My life, now fulfilled, looked onward to a bright future. I now knew His love. Like the Clark Sisters sang, "He gave me nothing to lose but all to gain." I felt like I had gained more than I could carry alone.

I was never meant to be held ransom inside, only to flow freely. The living water by which my tree was now planted allowed my deepest roots to drink and the fruit that I bore was refined.

Wisely allowing Him to be my landscaper, He pruned everything to perfection.

Calvary finally came to life, my mind going back to that hill as if I were there in the beginning. Watching the ultimate depiction of love, aside from the phenomenon we know to be the existence of man, I saw the nails in His hands and in His feet.

I saw His insides seeping out of the wounds as He hung, trying to support His body. He died a slow death as His lungs collapsed causing Him to eventually suffocate; the thorns so deep in His head that it burned from His own sweat. The smell of death so gripping that my stomach turned in thought.

The imagery was more than enough to capture for me what His blood means; His sacrifice of blood - each drop- brought me closer to my discovery, closer to my love, closer to eternity. Without the sacrifice of blood, I would be dead, cast away from the love I was designed to discover, lost in the midst of darkness, no light to pursue. The law, a constant reminder that I never measured up and I would forever be a slave to it. My Jesus was more bound than my imagery. As a slave to the law, I would have suffered until I too, suffocated to death.

It was love that lifted me out of where I had been, love that carried me when my legs gave way; love that poured out like blood so that I could say, *"He loves me!"*

"For God so Loved the World"

I find it so interesting how each day we live our lives slaves to a law that could never redeem us only to feel defeated and short of the glory we strive to achieve.

The love of God is so much more than the limitations we daily place upon it. "For God so loved the world..."[xi] are words that have a power as they are proclaimed but yet in our minds it really reads, "For God so loved the *SAINTS... Pastors...Missionaries...bishops etc.*" It's as if a title provides more love and acceptance, which is a contradiction to the existence of LOVE!

God has a passionate love for *ALL* of His creation. That means everything; the good, the bad and the ugly. If it were in essence more important to God for us to only live according to the law, then why did He send Christ to die?

1 John 4:1-9 says "This is how God showed his love among us: He sent his one and only Son into the world that we might live through him. This is love: not that we loved God, but that he loved us and sent his Son as an atoning sacrifice for our sins."[xii]

It is because the truism of God's heart does not lie in our daily religious rituals; it is based on the very thing He used to establish the world and that was His love.

I live my life now in light of the revelation that He loves me! It is by the preeminence of this love that I live daily pursuing more of His love and seeking to discover the mysteries of God Himself.

It is by this new mantra, *"Because He loved me first,"* that I live. I no longer do things in my life because they exist on my list of do's and don'ts, but solely out of a love relationship with Him.

Our relationship consists of us only having each other's reflections in our hearts. I want to reciprocate everything He has shown me and nothing short of it.

I live in the light of His love, pursuing to please Him not out of acceptance, but just out of pure love.

The very love He has shown me puts wind in my sails as I continue to discover more.

His love brings each page in His Word to life and I can gain new revelation as it is deposited and experienced.

His Word has become my 'daily bread, fulfilling a hunger only satisfied by divine delicacies that He feeds me. I am taking a taste from His hands, causing all hunger pains to cease.

My soul lives free, drinking of the living water that never runs dry. The living water nourishes and nurtures my pursuit and so I continue to press on, forward into eternity. I am not constrained by man's time. Hence, I press on continually being refined, so that one day I, too, can be clothed in Glory, not from man but in the presence of the One, who loved me first!

Epilogue

My journey and discovery is a never ending story. There will be no period to bring to a close everything that life reveals. There is no intention to only be captured in pages of a book. My journey exists as an account of the journey everyone will encounter with no one journey the same. The common denominator is the revelation of God's Heart!

I encourage you to look inside yourself and ask questions, questions that will lead you into a deeper discovery of who *you* are. Do not be mixed up by substitutes for what your heart really cries for…your heart cries for God!

Discovering Him is a life-long journey, full of abundant life, rivers of living water that quench an eternal thirst that nothing in this world can truly satisfy. The discovery is not bound to a denomination or an exclusionary rule that's based on how long you have been in relationship with God.

Many can walk with God all their life and never know the truth about His love. Embark on a journey that leaves a legacy so amazing and free that generations to come will seek it for themselves and one day eternally encounter it as you would have.

Lay aside any facades and masks; you owe it to yourself to be whole. The reflection in His heart is yours; His heart beats for you!

ENDNOTES

[i] John 15:13
[ii] John 3:16
[iii] Genesis 1:9-10
[iv] Mark 11:23 New American Standard Version 1995
[v] John 15:8
[vi] Philippians 3:13
[vii] Philippians 3:14
[viii] Luke 22:42
[ix] Ephesians 2:8 Weymouth New Testament
[x] 1 Corinthians 13:13
[xi] John 3:16
[xii] 1 John 4:9-10 New International Version

9 781615 790265